Sumner Welles

Seven Decisions That Shaped History

Harper & Brothers Publishers

NEW YORK

SEVEN DECISIONS THAT SHAPED HISTORY

FIRST EDITION

B-A

Books by Sumner Welles

THE TIME FOR DECISION

WHERE ARE WE HEADING?

SEVEN DECISIONS THAT SHAPED HISTORY

*

Seven Decisions
That Shaped History

To the Memory of

My Beloved Wife

At whose urgent insistence this book was written

Oxon Hill——Ouchy——Bar Harbor

Contents

Foreword   ix

Chapter I   "The Last Frail Chance . . ."   1

Chapter II   The Decision to Recognize the Vichy Government   31

Chapter III   Far Eastern Policy before Pearl Harbor   66

Chapter IV   The Decision that Saved New World Unity   94

Chapter V   The Decision to Postpone Political and Territorial Decisions until after the War   123

Chapter VI   Far Eastern Policy from Pearl Harbor to Hiroshima   146

Chapter VII   The United Nations Is Created before the War's End   172

Chapter VIII   Policy for Today   199

Index   232

Foreword

For the want of a nail the shoe was lost,
For the want of a shoe the horse was lost,
For the want of a horse the rider was lost,
For the want of a rider the race was lost,
For the want of a race the battle was lost,
For the want of a battle the kingdom was lost,
And all for the want of a horseshoe nail.

The reasons why a book has been written have often intrigued me. Partly because I believe others may share my curiosity, and still more to make clear my motives in writing this book, I offer this explanation of the genesis of *Seven Decisions That Shaped History*.

In October, 1948, I happened to meet Hamilton Fish Armstrong in New York. I have known Mr. Armstrong for many years. During the Second World War we worked closely together in the Department of State helping to draft the plan for what later became the United Nations Charter. Because of my admiration for the public service he has so long rendered as editor of *Foreign Affairs*, and for his exceptional knowledge of world affairs, his opinions always carry great weight with me.

I told him of my fear that some recent books giving grotesquely distorted versions of President Roosevelt's handling of many vital problems might so crystallize public opinion here and abroad that the subsequent writings of more impartial historians would not erase the initial impact of these smears. Mr. Armstrong shared my concern, but in lesser degree. I think it was his view that these books would defeat their own purpose, because of their obvious intemperance or malignancy. He suggested, however, that I write an article for *Foreign Affairs,* examining the whole field of President Roosevelt's wartime policy, and by citing chapter and verse, show how fantastic some of the falsehoods currently being published really were.

A few days later I received a letter from Mr. Armstrong telling me that on further thought he had reached the conclusion that what he had in mind was beyond the scope of a single article; but "that someone with real authority and inside knowledge should choose a number of points about which controversialists gather most thickly and deal with them seriatim." He was kind enough to say, "You are the obvious person to do this."

It is in no spirit of false modesty that I hasten to add that many of my colleagues in the Roosevelt Administration are as well fitted as I to undertake this task. Yet Mr. Armstrong's proposal was very appealing because of my conviction that the kind of examination he had in mind, if carried out by one whose advice on foreign policy President Roosevelt had sought, and who played some part in formulating that policy, would give the American people a chance to offset many of the myths that are being asked to credit against facts that are indisputable.

I am one of those who are convinced that the stature of Franklin D. Roosevelt will not shrink, but will rather grow, with the passage of years. The charges that his detractors started bringing even before the earth had settled on his grave will not in my opinion weaken the hold that his memory has upon the hearts of men and women who cherish human liberty. Nor will they, I think, ever lessen the deep impression that his administration has made upon the life of this republic and upon Western civilization.

Winston Churchill and Henry L. Stimson have given us their estimate of his quality and of his achievements as American Commander-in-Chief. The authority of such appraisals will scarcely be challenged by the impartial historian of tomorrow, particularly since they are shared by a great majority of the professionals in the armed services, who knew the predominant part President Roosevelt took in making the decisions that lead to ultimate victory.

It is rather in the field of foreign policy that I fear lasting harm may be done by some of the recent efforts to falsify the record made by President Roosevelt. Winston Churchill tells us of a conference at the Quai d'Orsay which he and Clement Attlee attended in the dark days of the spring of 1940. In urging upon the French leaders the need for last-ditch resistance, Mr. Attlee said that the very existence of democracy in Western Europe was at stake because Hitler did not confine himself to killing men; he also killed ideas.

The danger is that, by their attempt to blacken the character of the man whose memory they would assassinate, the Roosevelt-haters may also kill the ideas with which his name is associated.

The American people turned their backs upon isolation after the Japanese attack at Pearl Harbor and the Nazi and Fascist declarations of war upon the United States. The clear light of reason, intensified by the sacrifice of the lives of hundreds of thousands of young Americans and by the unparalleled expenditure of this country's resources, made it at last plain that the United States could no longer be safe in a world in which armed aggression was rampant. Most Americans were persuaded that for this nation there could be no true victory unless the end of the war brought with it a world in which the Four Freedoms would become realities; a world in which, through the United Nations, we would bear our full share of responsibility for preserving peace and advancing the welfare of mankind. But it is customary for human beings to experience a sense of revulsion after any acute emotional strain. That is peculiarly so with us in the United States. The urge to return to "normalcy" in the 1920's is but one example. There are many signs that a similar reaction is possible today, even as we fight the Communist aggressors in the Far East.

It is easy enough to discount some of the speeches delivered on the floor of the Senate or of the House of Representatives during the past year. I do not believe in fact that they represent more than a small sector of American opinion. But may not a considerable number of Americans be tempted to wonder, after reading the outpourings of such authors as the late Charles A. Beard or—in a very different category—John T. Flynn, whether President Roosevelt did not perhaps provoke the attack upon Pearl Harbor; whether he was not in fact hypnotized or flattered by Mr. Churchill into "pulling Britain's chestnuts out of the fire"; or whether actually he was not outsmarted by Stalin at Tehran and Yalta? And in that case, what I fear is that they may become correspondingly disheartened about our chances of ever succeeding in an international effort to build a free, a democratic, and a peaceful world order.

That is why I submitted Mr. Armstrong's proposal to my friend, Cass Canfield, the Chairman of the Board of Harper & Brothers. To my great satisfaction it commended itself to him. As in the case of my previous books, his suggestions have been invaluable. He is, in fact, responsible even for the title of this book.

But to Mr. Canfield as—the more I thought about it—to me, the more stimulating challenge the book offered was the opportunity to show how a number of decisions in which President Roosevelt had shared, and which had been made at crucial moments, had all, however unconnected they might seem to be, played a related part in determining the history of the decade of the Second World War as well as the history of the world for many generations to come.

After that I was for many months seriously ill and unable to begin the writing that had been so rapidly taking shape in my mind. This long period of seclusion nevertheless had its compensations. The present significance as well as the probable future consequences of the decisions which are the subject of this book have, I feel, been more justly evaluated as a result of that enforced immobility, which made it possible for me to concentrate on them.

It is, of course, true that the imponderables and the unforeseen cannot be ignored in formulating foreign policy. That is why a preventive war should always be regarded as an act of criminal folly. But the effects of the decisions of today upon the course of international relations tomorrow should not, therefore, be discounted. As Thomas Hardy so accurately puts it: "History . . . flows on like a thunderstorm-rill by a road side; now a straw turns it this way, now a tiny barrier of sand that."

In 1875 Prince Bismarck reached the conclusion that France was recovering far too rapidly from her defeat by Germany in 1871. She had not been "bled white" by the monetary indemnities exacted from her. She had, on the contrary, paid them off long before they were due. The injury to her national economy and to her security that the amputation of Alsace and Lorraine was intended to insure had not proved fatal; rather, it had aroused precisely that feeling of national unity which it had been Bismarck's chief purpose to prevent. In fact, France gave evidence of a national rebirth calculated to retain for her her historic position in the front rank of the major powers.

Bismarck determined upon a preventive war against France, intending this time to relegate her definitely to the category of a second-rate state. It is true that he was reluctantly compelled to abandon his project by the joint pressure of Russia and of a Great Britain that had not yet suffered the debilitating effects of a Baldwin or of a Ramsay MacDonald Cabinet. But Bismarck's decision burned into the consciousness of the French people a fear of Germany and a passion for the assurance of security that the defeat of 1871 could never alone have created. Reinforced in 1914 and 1939, these national motivations of the French have ever since been the chief obstacle to any viable European federation of which Germany becomes an equal member.

Bismarck's decision to conquer France only five years after the war he had forced upon her in 1870 has shaped the history of Europe, and consequently the history of the rest of the world, for seventy years. It has governed the thinking of the German people and has helped to make the German nation the peril to humanity that it has since become. It has directly affected the lives of people who never have had and who never will have the slightest knowledge that any such decision was ever made. In this same sense the decisions of which I write have played an incalculably important part in determining the future destinies of our civilization.

Granted that allowances must ever be made for the unexpected in human affairs, granted that the chances for success may have been as one in a hundred, it would, for example, be difficult to deny that the deliberate abortion by Mr. Chamberlain and Mr. Hull of President Roosevelt's decision in 1937 to use American influence to check the onrush of war in Europe may well have cost the world its last chance, in Winston Churchill's words, "to stave off, or even prevent, war."

When President Roosevelt was traveling on his war missions it was sometimes impossible to communicate with him for several days. The results would indeed have been far reaching had he been away from the White House on that dramatic night of January 25, 1942, when Mr. Hull insisted from Washington that I, as American delegate to the Inter-American Conference at Rio de Janeiro, demand that Argentina and Chile be outlawed and thereby break up the unity of the hemisphere, and had I consequently been unable to telephone the President and obtain his contrary decision.

Some of the more immediate consequences are hardly open to question. Because of its belief that a divergence between Argentine and Brazilian policies might tempt the Argentine military leaders to threaten Brazil's southern frontiers, the Brazilian Army would have opposed any break with the Axis. Ecuador, Peru, Bolivia and Paraguay would have found it expedient to follow Brazil's lead. The hemisphere would have been split into two camps. The pro-Axis influences in Argentina and in Chile would have been greatly strengthened, and the supporters of the United Nations in all South America would have been correspondingly weakened. It would have been impossible for the Government of Brazil, which wished to support the United States after Pearl Harbor, to offer this country the use of Brazilian ports and air bases. Those facilities were indispensable in carrying out the North African invasion of November, 1942. In that event, could the United States have occupied Morocco and Algeria soon enough to prevent Hitler from overrunning the whole of North Africa?

Groups of Nazi sympathizers, directed by Nazi agents, would have become increasingly powerful in all the South American republics; efforts to overthrow constitutional governments, like the attempt that so nearly succeeded in Bolivia, would have been engineered in many other countries, and the danger to our own safety would have been immeasurably increased.

From the long-range viewpoint inter-American solidarity might well have been destroyed for an indefinite period. And what would our hemispheric position now be in the light of our postwar contest with the Soviet Union?

In his reminiscences, Sir Edward Grey contends that events make diplomacy, instead of diplomacy making events. The essential fallacy in that generalization was never better shown up than by President Roosevelt's determination to obtain a functioning United Nations organization before the final victory. What would have happened had President Roosevelt not decided to employ every means within his power to secure the agreement of the Soviet Union and of Great Britain on the United Nations Charter before the defeat of the Axis? The United Nations has compelled the major powers to sit down and publicly discuss the conflicts of interest that have come to a head since 1945. It has made it possible for countries other than the Soviet Union and its satellites to co-operate in speeding reconstruction and rehabilitation, and, through regional systems of defense, to prepare the way for an international police power, without which world peace can never be maintained. It has provided the only mechanism that could keep alive the principles of international co-operation and of international justice. It has been the one factor that has so far prevented a hopelessly divided world.

Had President Roosevelt not devoted the last months of his life to getting a United Nations Charter before the collapse of Germany and Japan, war between the Soviet Union and the Western powers would already have been inevitable, and the fate of our civilization would today be trembling in the balance.

Every one of the other decisions listed in this book have, I believe, affected to a similar extent not only the history of our times, but the history of the world for many generations to come.

I have related in this volume several incidents that involve personalities. To these I have not previously referred. I have done so now because my conviction has grown stronger with the passage of the years that every aspect of American foreign policy should be laid objectively, but fully, before the American people.

The public in general still has the idea that foreign policy is carried on in an Olympian atmosphere. On the contrary, the foreign policy of a government, like the relations between two or more governments, has from time immemorial been as much affected by the consequences of selfish rivalries and petty jealousies and vanities as by honest differences on major issues. And so it is today in the conduct of American foreign policy. The more clearly the American people recognize that these factors have often governed the determination of their national policy and the policies of other countries, the better they will be able to understand the why and the wherefore of foreign relations.

That is the story of the origin of this book. It is not intended to be primarily a refutation of the charges of this or the other author. It is far from being an apology for an American administration that will never need an apology. It is an attempt by one who played a part in many of the events with which the book deals to offer the unvarnished truth about American decisions that did "shape history," and to show why those decisions so radically changed the pattern of our present and future lives.

Seven Decisions
That Shaped History

CHAPTER I

"The Last Frail Chance . . ."

IN A year when American GIs went to fight in Korea under the flag of the United Nations it is not easy to recapture our isolationist point of view in 1937.

We have now at last grasped the hardest of all the truths this nation has had to learn: however remote the aggression, however distant the social or economic disasters that afflict other peoples, sooner or later we ourselves will feel their impact. Twelve years ago most of us still imagined that the rapid disintegration of civilization that we were witnessing could have no effect upon the much-vaunted "American Way of Life."

Since Pearl Harbor the events that have crowded on us have surcharged our memories. Some of us, then serving in this Government, will always remember those years before the Second World War as a nightmare of impotence and of frustration.

The British and French refusal to move to halt aggression when Japan invaded China, when Mussolini attacked Ethiopia, when Hitler marched into the Rhineland, and when the Spanish Civil War became an international contest, had destroyed the League of Nations. Outside the New World men and women were beginning to lose faith in democracy.

Hope for collective security had gradually vanished. Great Britain and France had come to use the League of Nations as a mere instrument of their own policies. If any constructive approach to peace was made, as at Locarno, it was made outside the League. When Britain and France decided to follow the path of least resistance, as when Japan invaded China, it was not they that were blamed but the League. The League had become no more than a convenient scapegoat for a series of successful aggressions made inevitable by the blind selfishness of the great powers. We may not now like to remember it, but in 1937 only the Soviet Union still maintained that "peace is indivisible."

American abstention may well have been a chief cause of the League's failure. But that cannot palliate the abject record of France and Britain.

To the American admirer of Britain's long and glorious history there is no more painful chapter than that which covers the fifteen years beginning with Stanley Baldwin's rise to power in 1925. During that time a minority Labour Cabinet once came briefly to office. A fictitious "national government," of which Ramsay MacDonald was ostensibly Prime Minister, was maintained in Downing Street for some years. Behind the scenes Baldwin continued to reign supreme.

Before his advent British policy had for more than a century consistently comprised three major objectives: to maintain a balance of power in Europe so that Britain's influence would prove determining; to control the seas so that British trade would be safe throughout the world and the British Isles safe from blockade or invasion; and, finally, to maintain untrammeled freedom of communication between Britain and her dominions and colonies. Until the days of Baldwin, Britain had shown incomparable courage, vision and persistence in pursuing those three objectives. With Baldwin, Britain seemed even to forget what those objectives were.

Lloyd George must shoulder the responsibility for Britain's headlong demobilization after the First World War, and for the consequent inability of the Allies to enforce many of the provisions of the Versailles Treaty. But after the Nazis had gained control of Germany in 1933, Baldwin and his advisers were chiefly to blame for Germany's rearmament. At first, when co-operation with a willing France could readily have checked it, Stanley Baldwin, in the face of the facts Winston Churchill laid before the British people, denied that any rearming was going on. Later, when Goering and Goebbels were daily boasting that German rearmament was an accomplished fact, and when Germany's mighty air force could no longer be concealed, Baldwin rejected all demands for security measures because, he said, the British voter would back the party that stood for minimum military, naval and air budgets.

Britannia had become a shadow of her former self.

The defensive psychology that the Maginot Line had created in France had helped to undermine France's will to resist. An equilibrium between the Axis and the Western European powers could have been restored only by Russia's admission into the series of closely integrated military alliances that Louis Barthou had perfected while he was France's Foreign Minister and which his successor, Pierre Laval, allowed so rapidly to crumble. But the very thought of an alliance with Moscow was anathema to Baldwin and to the Tory and City spokesmen whose counsel he sought. The balance of power that Britain had persistently maintained since the Napoleonic Wars was gone. And there was no collective security to replace it.

The Anglo-German Naval Treaty of 1935 had understandably infuriated the French Navy and the bulk of French public opinion. Notwithstanding the prohibitions of the treaty, it was well known that new and powerful German submarines were being built. The superiority of Hitler's air power lessened the value of the British Navy, since in narrow waters naval vessels could readily be sunk by air attack. With Italy a German vassal, Britain could not even count herself secure in the Mediterranean or in the Suez Canal. Japan's growing ambitions in Asia rendered the British dominions and colonies in the Far East liable to an attack in force at any time.

These fifteen years also represent a dark era in the history of France's Third Republic.

Through the maze of gross corruption, of political scandal, and of petty partisan chicanery it is true that the figures of great men occasionally emerge—men who in less trying times would have left behind them a record of statesmanship and of patriotic accomplishment. But like the Constitution of the Fourth Republic today, the Constitution of the Third Republic made it all too easy for the national interest to be subordinated to individual or party interests and to the demands of the industrial monopolies.

When Hitler occupied the Rhineland in 1936 and thereby for the first time openly violated the Versailles Treaty, Pierre Étienne Flandin, the Foreign Minister, excused his failure to act (and we now know that determined action by France and Britain would have changed the entire history of the past thirteen years) on the ground that he could not obtain British support. It is true that support was refused. But can one conceive of a Clemenceau, a Poincaré, or even a Millerand fearing to take unilateral action when the safety of France was at stake?

The fatal maladies from which Britain and France were suffering were also afflicting the smaller European countries, although the symptoms in their case were less pronounced. Time and again the lesser powers tried to rescue the League of Nations from the ignominious role to which the major powers had relegated it. But as the years passed and their failure was apparent, the small countries became increasingly fearful of Axis might. And their national policies became correspondingly negative and timid.

The pressure that the Nazis brought to bear upon Rumania, Hungary, Yugoslavia and Bulgaria made them unwilling even to consider resistance to increasing German economic and political control when it was evident they could expect no support from England and France. Czechoslovakia alone still placed her faith in France. Poland was in the last stages of the deplorable Pilsudski dictatorship. Only Finland stood out as an example of a courageous and virile democracy.

The smaller European countries were afraid even to think of concerted action. Had they been willing to unite they could have made their voices heard. Driven by a contagious panic, they persuaded themselves that a return to the forms of the classic neutrality of the nineteenth century would bring them safety. With the collapse of the League there was in Europe no galvanizing force to arouse a will to collective defense. Only the United States could provide it.

In a positive American policy lay the sole remaining chance to prevent a world-wide war and social and political chaos. But what possibility was there that the American people or their Congress could be persuaded to approve any action by the Government that implied interference in world affairs?

American isolationism was still at its peak. The Harding,

Coolidge and Hoover administrations all had their share of responsibility. The well-intentioned but weirdly ingenuous paci-
fist organizations played no small part. The effort of the Nye
Committee to prove that wars are made only by munitions manufacturers and international bankers influenced far more millions
of Americans that most of us now recall. There was little
realization that if aggressive dictatorships marched on unchecked
Western civilization would come crashing down, and that the
United States could no more help suffering the consequences
than it could avoid sharing in the results of a collision between
the Earth and Mars.

At the outset of his first Administration, President Roosevelt
tried to pave the way for a universal reduction of armaments by
moving for an international agreement to define aggression.
There was much then, as there is now, to be said for the President's proposal. But the times were not propitious. It received
little public attention and much covert opposition from the
great powers. The stand he felt he had to take, for domestic
reasons, at the London Economic Conference in the spring of
1933, and the interpretation given to his subsequent "I hate
war" speech at Chautauqua convinced Europe that American
policy would continue to be as isolationist under the Roosevelt
Administration as it had been under the Republicans.

From the purely political standpoint, moreover, any move by
President Roosevelt to give American foreign policy even a suggestion of the international outlook it has today would have then
been political suicide. It would not only have been virulently
assailed by his partisan opponents, but it would have been
equally obnoxious to the leaders of the Democratic Party upon

whom the President was compelled to rely for the enactment of his legislative program.

And in 1937 most. Americans, Democrats or Republicans, honestly believed that there was danger in any policy of international collaboration to avert the conflict already so clearly foreshadowed. They thought, like the Swedes, the Dutch and the Swiss, and many other decent, honorable and peace-loving peoples, that the national safety could best be assured by an ostrich-like determination to refuse to see what was going on. They sought security in an illusory neutrality.

A few years before, when Henry L. Stimson, then President Hoover's Secretary of State, had sought with courage and with vision to employ American influence to check Japan's invasion of China, he had met with rebuffs from Great Britain and France. He had received only the most grudging acquiescence from Mr. Hoover. He had been unmercifully belabored in both houses of Congress. Except for a few leading newspapers in the East and on the Pacific coast he had received no support from the press.

President Roosevelt had been re-elected in the autumn of 1936 with the greatest Electoral College majority of any President since James Monroe. Yet the contest over his attempt to reform the Supreme Court had later provoked a schism within the Democratic Party as deep as it was bitter. The struggle that ensued undeniably alienated from Franklin Roosevelt some of the immense mass support that had been so clearly shown the preceding November.

Under the circumstances, the President was unwilling throughout that critical spring and summer of 1937 to make any new move that might provoke further public controversy, and thereby lessen the measure of popular confidence he still so largely retained. He did not speak out until October. During the intervening months he almost ostentatiously left the direction of foreign policy to Secretary Hull.

After my return from the Buenos Aires Conference of 1936, the President told me that he had decided to appoint me Under Secretary. Because of the enlarged scope of my responsibilities, I had more frequent chances than before to talk alone with the President in his office or in his White House study. And on occasion during the hot months he would drive out to have dinner at my house in the country. At such times we talked more and more often of the growing collapse of world law and order, of the looming dangers in Hitler's and Mussolini's policies, and of the perils to the United States in Japan's invasion of China.

The President was fully alive to the future menace to the United States in any direct or indirect domination of Europe by Nazi Germany. But I wish to make it unmistakably plain that in 1937 he was far more preoccupied with the threat represented by Japan.

It was in the early part of that same summer that he first talked to me of the possibility of erecting a naval barrier, later to be spoken of as a "quarantine," if Japan should persist in her policy of conquering the rest of Asia.

On July 16, 1937, Secretary Hull circularized all the governments of the world with a note asking that they subscribe to a pledge based upon the following "Eight Pillars of Peace," of which he was particularly proud, and which he had proclaimed to humanity at the Buenos Aires Conference the preceding December:

1. People must be educated for peace. Each nation must make itself safe for peace.
2. Frequent conferences between representatives of nations, and intercourse between their peoples, are essential.
3. The consummation of the five well-known peace agreements will provide adequate peace machinery. (These included the Kellogg Pact and the Saavedra Lamas Antiwar Pact.)
4. In the event of war in this hemisphere, there should be a common policy of neutrality.
5. The nations should adopt commercial policies to bring each that prosperity upon which enduring peace is founded.
6. Practical international co-operation is essential to restore many indispensable relationships between nations and prevent the demoralization with which national character and conduct are threatened.
7. International law should be re-established, revitalized, and strengthened. Armies and navies are no permanent substitute for its great principles.
8. Faithful observance of undertakings between nations is the foundation of international order, and rests upon moral law, the highest of all law.

In his note Mr. Hull added:

Any situation in which armed hostilities are in progress or are threatened is a situation wherein rights and interests of all nations either are or may be seriously affected. There can be no serious hostilities anywhere in the world which will not one way or another affect interests or rights or obligations of this country.

Naturally enough no government expressed any public dissent. For the Axis dictators to have said they disagreed at a time when they were doing their utmost to lull the fears of the neighbors whom they were so soon to attack, would have been tantamount to a criminal's telling the local policeman of his intentions to rob and murder his neighbors.

I remember that Mr. Hull was exceedingly irritated because the British Government delayed its reply, and that when it was at length received it was decidedly reserved. I suspect that Mr. Eden, who was still Mr. Chamberlain's Foreign Secretary, saw as little of practical value to be gained in signing the proffered pledge as in officially reaffirming the validity of the Beatitudes.

Such a communication from the American Government at that determining moment in world affairs merely convinced the dictators that the United States would limit its interference to words. It persuaded the handful of leaders of the Western democracies who were still frantically seeking to arouse their peoples to the need for concerted measures of defense that Washington's appraisal of the European situation was so grossly unrealistic as to rule out all hope of tangible support there.

It was not that the contents of Mr. Hull's note were not on the whole unassailable. Except for his third Pillar of Peace, the American circular stated truths that were not open to question. For centuries past, in one form or another, the same principles had been repeatedly proclaimed, and frequently in infinitely more eloquent and moving terms, as those to which mankind must adhere, if a peaceful world were ever to exist. The trouble was that mankind had never yet been willing to sweat and sacrifice sufficiently to bring that world into being.

What was needed in 1937 was not a further reiteration of principles that had been reiterated time and again even since the Treaty of Versailles. What was needed, on the contrary, was some clear indication that the United States was willing to act in order to try to prevent war in Europe, and thus save those principles from oblivion.

Mr. Hull was a member of that diminishing group of twentieth-century liberals who followed the path traced by Richard Cobden. As John Morley once justly said, the new currents of thought on property, wealth and the rights of man for which Cobden was responsible have supplied both Conservatives and Liberals alike with working principles and fighting watchwords, not for one generation, but for the better part of two. The measure of Cobden's accomplishment has never yet been sufficiently appreciated. It was in no small way owing to the liberal economic tenets that he persuaded his fellow countrymen to accept that the British Empire by the end of the nineteenth century had become the arbiter of the world's destiny, and that the twentieth century dawned in an atmosphere of peace, of slow but steady improvement in social conditions, and of unparalleled material prosperity.

Mr. Hull was Cobden's worthy disciple. The Trade Agreements Act of 1934, for which he was solely responsible, was as much a landmark as was Cobden's Anglo-French Commercial Treaty concluded seventy-five years before. It struck a note of economic sanity when it was most needed. Even under the altogether abnormal conditions in which it operated, it was of material benefit to the United States and to the other co-operating nations.

The tragedy was, of course, that while during the decades when Cobden preached and worked the peoples of the earth were witnessing the gradual substitution of freedom for force in the government of men, in the decades after the First World War we were seeing the process reversed. After the Soviet Revolution the concept of the totalitarian state had an undeniable appeal to many Liberals because of their delusion that the social injustices which tarnished even the most advanced democracies could be cured only by statism. In such an atmosphere economic freedom could no more prosper than could political freedom.

Given the transformation that the world has undergone during the past half century, mankind can never again return to an economic regime as free from government intervention as that in which Cobden believed. The obvious benefits which peoples derive from some forms of government control over their national economy, such as those prescribed by the United Nations, must presage, even to those die-hards most wedded to the shibboleth of "free enterprise," a lasting departure from the free economic life of the nineteenth century.

Secretary Hull's discourses to the foreign diplomats whom he received and to his associates in the State Department always reminded me irresistibly of the story of the Civil War politician whose speeches—more notable for their length than for their content—were once likened to a train with twenty cars from which emerged but a single passenger. In Mr. Hull's trains the passenger was always the same—the Trade Agreements Program. Until the outbreak of the war in 1939 he seemed to believe that what he termed "preachments" to foreign governments, together with the series of trade agreements for which he so ably worked, would be sufficient to halt the triumphal march of the dictators and to bring the world back to paths of virtue and peace. But no matter how beneficial a liberal economic regime might have been in more normal times, after 1936 no economic remedy could have dissipated the political and military threats that confronted all the democracies. This Mr. Hull seemed unable to understand.

President Roosevelt's famous "quarantine" speech, delivered in Chicago early in October, 1937, expressed a totally different point of view. It was something you could get your teeth into.

I had returned from a brief trip to Europe only a few days before. I had no share in suggesting any part of its text. But because of the talks I had had with the President during the summer, the term "quarantine," as well as the purposes that lay behind it, were familiar to me.

I was enthusiastic about the speech. I so told the President when I first saw him after he came back from Chicago. It was apparent that he was dismayed by the widespread violence of the attacks his speech had already provoked. He was equally surprised by the failure of some of the more prominent members of the Administration vigorously and effectively to back the stand he had taken. No skilled politician—and Franklin Roosevelt was consummately skilled—would under those circumstances have involved himself in detailed explanations or efforts to reply to the fantastic distortions of his proposals. He hoped, I think, that the shock the country had experienced would in the long run prove tonic, and that many millions of Americans would obtain from his Chicago speech a more realistic understanding of the kind of world that was already closing in on the United States.

I never have made, and I do not now make, any claim to special prescience during the years before the Second World War. I did not foresee the rapidity with which the climax came. I doubted in the autumn of 1937 that the German General Staff would ever permit Hitler to wage a world war so long as the Soviet Union was Germany's declared foe. I did not then foresee the possibility of an understanding between Moscow and Berlin. Short of any such development I believed that the Western powers of Europe could still become a match for even a rearmed Germany.

But no one in the position I then occupied in the Department of State and who had the chance to talk each summer with many of Europe's leading statesmen, could have failed to be profoundly pessimistic about the future. Nor could there be any doubt about the danger to the United States and the rest of the New World if war broke out in Europe.

I remember very well one of the first talks I had with the President after my return that year from my European vacation. I found him far more preoccupied with the trend in world affairs than he had been before. We discussed one evening in his room in the White House offices what, if anything, the United States could do. There seemed no longer to be even the slightest possibility that either England or France would take a firm stand. I recall that we discussed the pusillanimous role that both had so far played in the Spanish Civil War. (It must be sadly admitted that the part of the United States was no more courageous.) The President was especially incensed over the official farce that the submarines in the Mediterranean attacking ships carrying supplies to the Spanish Republics were "of unknown nationality," when every man and woman in Western Europe was well aware that they were Italian.

I told the President that I had some rough ideas which were gradually taking shape in my mind. There was a step he might take that would perhaps be of practical benefit and which would not be opposed by the Congress and public opinion. Once I had worked it out, I said, I would talk it over with Mr. Hull and then bring it over some evening to the White House for his consideration.

The major objective was clear. That was to make it plain to Germany, Italy and Japan that the United States could not remain indifferent if they persisted in preparing for world conquest. They must learn that, should a new war break out, the United States knew she could not avoid sharing in its disastrous consequences and might well be compelled to join in protective measures against the aggressor governments.

A further purpose was to arouse the will to resist of the peoples of the European democracies, large and small. Nothing could do this so well as a clear-cut indication that the United States would lend a hand in an international effort to resolve the mounting crisis.

The obstacles and the pitfalls were quite as plain. Germany and Japan would never be diverted from the present course until they became convinced that the isolationists were not going to be able to veto a positive American foreign policy. It would be futile to appeal to international law or to justice in the case of such a criminal paranoiac as Hitler or such a shameless international blackmailer as Mussolini. Only fear that the military and productive strength of the United States might, as in 1917, be thrown into the scales against them, would induce them to call a halt.

Another handicap would be Mr. Chamberlain's faith in his own powers as an amateur Foreign Secretary. It was highly improbable that the British Government would abandon its policy of bilateral appeasement negotiations with the dictators.

There was no slightest ground for optimism concerning French policy.

✶ It would be a bad blunder for the President even to think of calling an international conference. Europe itself was sick of conferences. The breakdown in the London Economic Conference of 1933, the collapse of all efforts to limit military or naval armaments, and the failure to which the coming Brussels Conference on the Far East was so patently foredoomed, had been more than enough to disgust the America people with the very words "international conference."

Yet there must still be something positive that Washington could do. Surely it was this country's most sacred obligation to try to save the world and its own sons from a new world war.

Armistice Day was only a month off. The tragedy and the hideous futility of war never hit me more directly than during those yearly rites performed in so many far-flung lands at the grave of the Unknown Soldier. I believed that the President could have no better opportunity to summon the peoples of the world to a new crusade for peace than on that Memorial Day to appeal for a vast international effort to avoid war before it was too late.

As the project gradually crystallized in my mind it had two separate and wholly distinct phases.

The first was admittedly an effort to appeal to human emotion and to moral courage throughout the world. I thought that after the customary Armistice Day ceremonies the President, without prior notice, so as to prevent leakage, might summon to the White House all the diplomatic representatives in Washington. He would ask them to tell their governments that he, as President of the United States, had unhappily concluded that unless the nations of the world, and particularly the major powers, returned to those basic standards of international law which Western civilization had gradually and painfully evolved, there was scant likelihood that world peace could be preserved. He would say he was prepared to have many people assert that because attempts to safeguard world order had failed in the past any new effort must now also fail. But he refused to admit that mankind cannot progress, nor could he let such pessimism justify a failure to make every effort for peace of which he as President of the United States was capable.

He would emphasize the fact that armaments were consuming an ever larger percentage of each country's productive capacity and that the resulting immense tax burdens were holding down living standards everywhere and retarding social progress. It seemed to him essential, he would say, that an international exchange of views be immediately arranged in the hope of working out an agreement by which armaments would each year be progressively reduced, the natural resources of the earth be utilized for the common benefit rather than for common destruction, and the increasing obstacles to normal trade between all peoples be simultaneously lessened.

He would ask all governments to reach an agreement as soon as possible upon the essential principles of international conduct and upon the best means of insuring their observance; upon the best ways to obtain a real reduction in armaments as well as some way to make certain that humanitarian rules would be observed if war should nevertheless break out; and finally, on a way to insure all peoples equal treatment and opportunity in their economic relations.

The President would conclude his Armistice Day appeal with the assurance that should his suggestion be accepted, the United

States would immediately ask a few other governments to join with it in drawing up tentative proposals which all governments could then consider as a basis for a universal agreement.

The second part of the project was wholly concrete. If his Armistice Day proposal was accepted the President would immediately invite nine other nations—for the most part smaller countries, not yet involved in the European or Asiatic contests, but representing all regions—to join with the United States in drawing up an agenda covering the chief points mentioned in his address. From there on this Executive Committee, working in Washington with the United States, would maintain the necessary communication with all the other governments until a final conclusion was reached.

In the light of American foreign policy today such a proposal seems so tenuous as to be no more than a palliative. But remember the moment in which it was formulated.

It was my hope that because no military commitments, direct or indirect, were involved, and because the purpose was primarily to use American influence to arrest a collapse of international law and of world order, the proposal would receive the support of Congress and of a majority of the American people.

From another standpoint it had these immense practical advantages.

The Axis powers could only regard it as a warning that the United States saw clearly the dangers inherent in their policies and, for the first time since the First World War, was prepared to interject her influence into European affairs to try to check further Axis expansion.

It would rally and unite those most decent members of the family of nations like Norway, Denmark, Sweden, Finland and the Low Countries, as well as Czechoslovakia and several of her eastern neighbors, by giving them tangible hope that peace was not yet lost. It would check the flight toward isolation and an illusory neutrality. It would not be opposed by the Soviet Union.

All the other American republics would enthusiastically support the move, not only because of its intrinsic merits but also because it was initiated by a President of the United States in whom they had come to place unlimited confidence. It would encourage the sorely stricken people of China.

It would be welcomed by the peoples of the major European democracies. Those were the times when ten million British men and women were in a popular referendum voting their faith in the League of Nations and in the great principles of international co-operation for collective security. Those were the days when millions of Frenchmen like millions of Americans were feverishly embracing all manner of fantastic peace schemes solely because no saner or sounder plan to prevent war was offered.

Finally, a move of this kind by America would without any doubt strengthen the backbone of that overwhelming majority of the Italian people who secretly opposed the bellicose policies of their Duce, and of those Germans who detested or perhaps distrusted Hitlerism.

For the better part of a week I spent all my free time concentrating on the problem.

The project finally resolved itself into three separate documents to be submitted to the President.

The first was the appeal to the world on Armistice Day. The second was the agenda to be proposed by the United States to the countries chosen as members of the original Executive Committee. The third document was the list of the countries forming that committee. It included representatives of Latin America, of the smaller countries of Europe, and of the Near and Far East.

On the first Sunday after finishing this draft, I asked Norman Davis to come to talk over the project with me.

Norman Davis occupied a unique position in the Roosevelt Administration, although his only full-time office was Chairman of the American Red Cross. Roosevelt and he had both been members of the "Little Cabinet" during the Wilson Administration. He was never one of the President's most intimate friends, but the President had great confidence in his judgment and gave, I know, some thought to appointing him Secretary of State when his Cabinet was being chosen early in 1933. Norman Davis had already been named American delegate to the Brussels Conference on the Far East due to meet within a few weeks. Having served as American representative in innumerable other international conferences under Republican and Democratic Administrations alike, he had an exceptionally comprehensive grasp of foreign affairs and had won to a singular degree the respect, the confidence, and the personal liking of Europe's leading statesmen. He was himself a far-sighted, constructive and conciliatory statesman in the truest sense of the term.

From the time when he had been Under Secretary of State in 1920, and I had served under him as a very junior officer, he had been one of my most loyal and devoted friends. I shall always be profoundly grateful to him for the advice and help he gave me without stint until his premature death in 1944.

In the present instance Norman Davis had a further qualification that was of still greater significance. There was no man in whom Secretary Hull imposed greater confidence. They both came from Tennessee. During the many barren years in which

Mr. Hull, as a minority Congressman, had battled in the House of Representatives against the Republican high tariff, Norman Davis had been one of his staunchest supporters. Later, when a major question of foreign policy came up for consideration Norman Davis's influence on Mr. Hull often proved to be conclusive. I was sure now that, if Norman Davis favored the proposal I had in mind, he could clarify its basic objectives for the Secretary of State. After a very long talk, during which we went over every possible ramification, including the effect of a new presidential move upon American public opinion in the light of the Chicago "quarantine" speech, I found to my great satisfaction that Norman Davis agreed wholeheartedly and enthusiastically with the objectives and methods I had in mind. He said he saw no other way in which the Administration could helpfully exercise American influence in Europe and the Far East and be reasonably assured of the backing of the American people.

We agreed that I would take up the project with Mr. Hull the following day and that Norman Davis would either be with him at the time I talked with him or immediately thereafter.

I thereupon submitted the entire plan to Mr. Hull, doing my best to make it clear that two separate steps were involved. The first was an attempt by President Roosevelt to galvanize the emotional and moral fervor of the Western world in behalf of the imperative need to preserve peace, and to indicate that the United States was prepared to accept leadership in a movement to halt the drift toward war. The second step was not, of course, a proposal for a peace conference, but offered a practical method by which a small group of peace-loving nations, headed by the United States, could work to make peace a reality.

While it would be too much to say that Secretary Hull evinced any intense interest in the project, he most certainly made no objection. I told him that in my conversation with the President I had said that I would submit the project to him as soon as I had talked it over with the Secretary of State. Secretary Hull expressed no desire that I should not do so.

I then discussed the project with the President in every detail. He was not only receptive, but particularly enthusiastic. It was always a joy to work with Franklin Roosevelt. His mind grasped so rapidly all the implications of a new proposal, no matter how vast its scope, that crossing the t's and dotting the i's were usually unnecessary.

After our discussion, he summed up the entire matter in a few words. He said the plan would give him the opportunity to appeal for the support of the American people and all the other democratic peoples in a new attempt to maintain peace. At the same time, he said, it would show the European dictators that the United States was not so indifferent to their plans for world domination as they had been led to believe.

He talked over at great length the ceremony to be held in the East Room of the White House on Armistice Day, even debating the best way to keep confidential his reasons for inviting the foreign Ambassadors to meet with him that afternoon. The best plan, he thought, would be for him to send individual invitations to each Ambassador on the morning of Armistice Day. He liked the draft that I submitted to him as a suggestion for the appeal he would make at the White House conference. He immediately started to write into the text words and sentences of his own as they occurred to him, and finally told me that he would keep the draft with him and let me have it back with the changes he wished made within a day or so.

It was, consequently, with a sense of profound discouragement that I learned from Norman Davis the next day that Secretary Hull's original tepid acquiescence had changed to violent opposition to the whole idea. Mr. Davis said it seemed impossible to persuade Mr. Hull that the White House meeting would not be a "peace congress"; and that after his burning at the London Economic Conference of 1933 Mr. Hull was twice shy of any international gathering. He also told me that Mr. Hull insisted that the British Cabinet headed by Mr. Chamberlain should in any event be consulted first, and thereafter several other governments. Needless to say—and events later so proved—the British Government would use every means at its disposal to block the President's move if it were forewarned. Prior consultation would ruin every chance of achieving the desired aims in this first attempt to wake the democracies to the need for action.

The account that Mr. Hull gives of this episode in his own book of reminiscences makes it clear that Norman Davis's interpretation of his point of view was in every detail accurate. Mr. Hull says "When I found that the President was all for going ahead with the Armistice Day drama in the White House, I earnestly argued against the project as being illogical and impossible." He says further: "It would be fatal to lull the democracies into a feeling of tranquillity through a peace congress at the very moment when their utmost efforts should actually be directed toward arming themselves for self-defense."

Nothing like "a peace congress" was even remotely considered by the President. Far from desiring "to lull the democracies into a feeling of tranquillity" the exact reverse was his intent. He was convinced that in making this concrete proposal he would be taking the most effective step possible to arouse them to a feeling of *intranquillity*. If the Axis governments refused to co-operate, nothing would be better calculated to convince the democracies that isolation and neutrality in the modern world could never insure their safety.

The President told me at once of the protests to which he had been subjected by his Secretary of State. I did my utmost during those last days of October to dispel Mr. Hull's misunderstanding. He, however, made it plain that his mind was fixed and that he was unwilling to discuss the project any further.

One must appreciate the President's dilemma. He had met with a far more general national rebuff than he had anticipated after his "quarantine" speech only a few weeks before. His Secretary of State, who had cautiously refrained from publicly supporting him at that time, unquestionably held in his conduct of foreign policy a measure of popular confidence that the President himself was not destined to secure for some time. If the President went ahead on Armistice Day with a project that his Secretary of State made it evident—through the handful of newspaper correspondents who, unknown to the public, often served to further his views—he thought was "illogical and impossible," the effect upon public opinion at home would have been disastrous. The President's political opponents would at once have seized the chance to distort his purpose and confuse the issues. Without general support at home all the benefits sought abroad would have been sacrificed. About the end of October the President told me that he felt he had no alternative but to abandon the plan.

I shall never forget the morning of that Armistice Day of 1937. I have regretted few things so much as that an opportunity which Franklin Roosevelt was so singularly qualified to grasp should thus have so needlessly been thrown away.

Neither the President, Mr. Hull, nor I made any further reference to the project for some weeks.

Upon his return from Brussels, Norman Davis immediately set about to convince Mr. Hull that even though the time factor now ruled out the first part of the plan, the United States should still take steps to carry out the second part. Whatever the reasons may have been, he was now, at least to some extent, successful.

Shortly after New Year's Day, 1938, Mr. Hull told me that he had decided to withdraw his opposition to the second part of my proposal, and that if the President wished to proceed along those lines he would not object. His proviso, however, and upon this he was adamant, was that Mr. Chamberlain must be consulted, and should he agree, then France, Germany and Italy, before any move was made by the White House. I found it impossible to convince him of what to me seemed the glaringly obvious dangers in that course. I said that Mr. Chamberlain had already taken all the reins of British foreign policy into his own hands, and that his notorious purpose was to negotiate bilaterally with Germany and Italy. For the United States to make its move dependent upon Mr. Chamberlain's consent, and contingently upon a green light from Berlin and Rome, was to court disaster if we wanted any practical results. To this argument I added that with the moral and emotional impact of the move already lost, if we were now to have any chance whatever for success the project must be launched without prior warning. We needed public opinion strongly behind us, and public opinion so widespread and so enthusiastic that no government could afford to refuse to co-operate. The leakage of confidential information from Downing Street in those days was notorious. If the British Government had advance notice, there was every likelihood that the whole story would be in the press within forty-eight hours. In that case the proposal would be subject to every kind of misinterpretation before the President could explain it to the American people. None of my arguments had the slightest effect.

When I talked the problem over with the President on January 11 I found him harassed and irritated by Mr. Hull's persistent objections. Nevertheless he said that, slim as the chances now were that we could get any practical benefits from the remnants of a proposal which, he repeated, might in its original form have had some possibility of success the preceding November, he felt it to be his solemn duty to try out any such plan to preserve peace. We agreed upon a revised version of the original proposal, to be sent by him to other governments, and drafted a covering message to be sent first of all in his own name to Mr. Chamberlain.

In order to avoid all possibility of publicity I telephoned the British Ambassador, Sir Ronald Lindsay, and asked if I could come to see him at his Embassy late in the afternoon of the same day. Sir Ronald Lindsay was a towering Scot little given to effusion or to any display of emotion. His great service to the cause of Anglo-American co-operation during the critical years of his mission in Washington has never been sufficiently recognized. He was aloof and reserved. He was by no means a favorite of the press. But he was a man of wide experience and of deep understanding, with an unshakable faith in the verities of Anglo-Saxon civilization. In the last years of his life the conviction grew upon him that Western civilization could be saved only if those verities were preserved, and that their preservation was doubtful without intimate collaboration between the English-speaking peoples.

The Ambassador received me in his study. He placed the

documents I handed him upon his standing desk. I can see him now in the winter twilight reading with growing interest the typewritten sheets I had given him. At length he said with profound emotion, "This is the first hope I have had in more than a year that a new world war can be prevented."

In *The Gathering Storm* Winston Churchill says that Sir Ronald Lindsay told Mr. Chamberlain in his telegram "that in his view the President's plan was a genuine effort to relax international tension and that if His Majesty's Government withheld their support, the progress that had been made in Anglo-American co-operation during the previous two years would be destroyed." He adds that Sir Ronald Lindsay urged in the most earnest manner that the President's proposal be accepted.

As I have already said in my own book, *The Time for Decision*, the reply that came from Mr. Chamberlain was like "a douche of cold water." He expressed the belief that Germany and Italy would take advantage of the President's proposal to put off negotiating a settlement between the Axis and Great Britain and France; he was convinced such a settlement was essential "if appeasement were to be achieved"; he feared that the Axis dictators might be led to make demands even greater than those at which they had already hinted. Mr. Chamberlain recommended that the President defer any steps to carry out the plan he had in mind. In the meanwhile Mr. Chamberlain said he would keep him informed of his own negotiations.

We all now know that owing to the insistence of Mr. Eden, who hurried back to London from a vacation in France, a series of Cabinet meetings were held. At the end of January Mr. Chamberlain sent new messages to the President, which while more cordial, made it plain that he feared the chief effect of the President's proposal would be to irritate Germany and Italy as well as Japan.

The tides had by then swept too far. It was futile for the President to continue with the project. Within two weeks Hitler made his demands upon the Chancellor of Austria. A month later the Austrian Republic was annexed to the Nazi Reich. From that time on no step by the United States short of armed support of the Western European democracies would have prevented war.

Mr. Churchill, I believe, does not yet know the earlier part of this story. He therefore logically places the responsibility for the scuttling of the American proposal upon Mr. Chamberlain. He remarks:

> That Mr. Chamberlain, with his limited outlook and inexperience of the European scene, should have possessed the self-sufficiency to wave away the proffered hand stretched out across the Atlantic leaves one, even at this date, breathless with amazement.[1]

As we look back from the perspective of history, and with full knowledge of the official archives of the Nazi Government, now in the possession of the United States, there can be little question that the autumn of 1937 offered the last chance to prevent the Second World War. From evidence produced at the Nuremberg trials, it is known that at a meeting with his chief advisers six days before Armistice Day, 1937, Hitler told them that Austria and Czechoslovakia must be seized before 1943-1945. Is there any reasonable doubt that if he had not been convinced that the United States would disinterest itself completely from the fate of Europe he would not then have made that decision? Is there

---

[1] Churchill, Winston, *The Gathering Storm* (Boston: Houghton Mifflin Co., 1948), p. 255.

any ground for doubt that he moved up the date for the seizure of Austria to March, 1938, quite as much because he believed the United States would make no further attempt to stem his aggression against the rest of Europe as because of the appeasement policies of Britain and France?

In his book Mr. Hull sneers at the plan for the Armistice Day White House meeting as "pyrotechnics." What the meeting would in reality have been was no more nor less than an effort to mobilize the power of public opinion throughout the world—even in Germany and Italy—behind the President's endeavor to prevent the drift toward war.

In his memoirs Mr. Hull says most revealingly of the reasons for his opposition:

It seemed to me thoroughly unrealistic, just at the time when we needed to arouse public opinion to the dangers abroad and the necessity to rearm to meet those dangers, to turn away from thoughts of self-defense and undertake to revive a completely collapsed movement. To have pursued a theory so credulous would have played into the hands of the Axis as completely as did the later neutrality policies of Belgium and Holland.

He then adds:

Furthermore, the peaceful minded nations would have gravitated much further than they had into a policy of appeasement, probably under the leadership of our friend, Prime Minister Chamberlain.

(Yet it was this same Prime Minister Chamberlain who, Mr. Hull insisted, should be given a veto power over the President's suggested peace initiative!)

At this point a comparison may be valuable.

If there is one man in the democracies of Western Europe who stands out above all others as having never for an instant turned away "from thoughts of self-defense," and who never ceased his efforts "to arouse public opinion to the dangers abroad and the necessity to rearm to meet those dangers," it is surely Winston Churchill.

Compare Mr. Hull's estimate of the plan that President Roosevelt so earnestly wished to carry out with Mr. Churchill's appraisal.

In *The Gathering Storm* Winston Churchill writes:

No event could have been more likely to stave off, or even prevent, war than the arrival of the United States in the circle of European hates and fears. To Britain it was a matter almost of life and death. No one can measure in retrospect its effect upon the course of events in Austria and later at Munich. We must regard its rejection—and such it was—as the loss of the last frail chance to save the world from tyranny otherwise than by war.[2]

The responsibility for the loss of this last "frail chance" to spare humanity the greatest of all recorded catastrophes can be laid at the doors only of two men—Neville Chamberlain and Cordell Hull. It was their decision that was determining.

And as we look over this devastated world, recognize the dangers and uncertainties we now confront, and recall the tragedy, misery and suffering of the past decade, even if there was but one chance in a million for success, was that chance not worth taking?

[2] *Ibid.*, p. 254.

CHAPTER II

The Decision to Recognize the Vichy Government

PRESIDENT ROOSEVELT'S decision to maintain diplomatic relations with the Vichy Government from the time
of France's downfall in June, 1940, until North Africa was
liberated two years later proved to be one of the most bitterly
controversial issues raised by his conduct of our foreign relations.
It was decried by many of our ablest commentators, even by those
who strongly supported the President. It provoked recurrent
storms of hysterical abuse both here and in Great Britain. It
called forth a degree of vituperation rarely equaled in the history
of American foreign policy.

Now that ten years have passed since Marshal Pétain sued
Hitler for an armistice, few of us remember how violent were
the passions that policy aroused. Still fewer of us have had much
chance to learn how largely the propaganda of the Free French,
backed by several agencies of the British Government, together
with the propaganda of the Communist Party, was responsible
for the failure of the American people to understand the why and
the wherefore of the Vichy policy.

Columnists and editors of the more liberal stripe played their
part in inflaming popular sentiment. But it was chiefly foreign-
inspired propaganda, working on the emotions of people who

loathed Nazi Germany and who were deeply sympathetic to France's plight, that prevented them from seeing what the stakes really were. Had the President between 1940 and 1942 spelled out from the White House his real reasons for the Vichy policy, the warning thus given the Nazi leaders would have defeated the very purposes for which the policy had been adopted. Yet under more normal conditions the President's objectives should have been plain to most Americans.

To quote an analysis I offered a State Department press conference in 1942, "American diplomacy has been forced to undertake what is not a very gratifying role, not a very agreeable role and not a very sympathetic role, that is to fight a rear guard action."

Within the last two years two authoritative books, Admiral Leahy's *I Was There* and Professor William L. Langer's *Our Vichy Gamble*, have dealt fully with the Vichy policy. They prove, I think, that any other policy would have endangered Anglo-American control of the Atlantic before as well as after Pearl Harbor, and would have gravely jeopardized the success of the North African invasion.

This chapter is intended primarily to supplement those two books. I hope it may throw some additional light on the reasons for the Vichy policy and on its results.

In July of 1940 very few of us in Washington believed that Britain, even under Winston Churchill's inspired leadership, could long hold out against Nazi Germany. The entire Atlantic coast as far as the Spanish frontier was in Hitler's hands. We knew that Hitler would try to make a deal with Franco. If he succeeded, Hitler would seize Gibraltar, close the western entrance to the Mediterranean and extend his control to North

Africa. If Britain fell, all the vast resources of Western Europe would be in Nazi hands. The threat to the safety of the United States was acute.

What was paramount in Roosevelt's mind was the security of the British and French fleets. With the major part of our own navy necessarily concentrated in the Pacific, continued Anglo-American supremacy in the Atlantic was his primary concern. Were Hitler to obtain the bulk of the French fleet, that supremacy would be ended.

It was true that Hitler did not, as most of us expected, refuse to negotiate with Pétain, nor did he proceed to occupy all of France together with her North African territories. It was true that the terms of the armistice granted Marshal Pétain were unexpectedly lenient. They not only permitted the French to keep most of their navy, but they also permitted the Vichy Government to exercise nominal authority in some two-fifths of France's metropolitan territory, and an even greater measure of authority in North Africa.

We did not then know what the German archives have since revealed. Hitler had guessed wrong. He had not prepared for the invasion of England because he was convinced that after France's downfall England would be forced to sue for peace. He believed that lenient armistice terms would persuade France to collaborate with Germany in her attempt to dominate the world, and to become a willing satellite in the Nazi Europe that he was determined to create. We did know, however, that Hitler's failure to occupy France and North Africa and to seize the French Navy gave us an opportunity to make his tactics serve our own ends.

Roosevelt decided he would try to keep the Vichy Government from consenting to Hitler's use of any French naval vessels against Britain, and from agreeing to any German encroachment upon French authority in North Africa. He wanted to make it clear that the United States intended to enforce the resolution adopted by all the American republics at Havana in 1940 that no Western hemisphere territories held by a non-American power might be transferred to any other non-American power.

Those were the major objectives of American diplomacy in our dealings with the Vichy Government.

It would be too much to say that the President was able in the early autumn of 1940 to see clearly what the political trends in France were going to be. The French domestic situation was essentially one of confusion worse confounded.

Upon his return to the United States at the end of July the former American Ambassador to France had announced to the press: "Marshal Pétain is universally respected in France. . . ." He "has a tremendous reputation and is thoroughly honest and straightforward. Pétain is absolutely the boss." There seemed at that time little reason to quarrel with this analysis. The old Marshal was the almost legendary "hero of Verdun" of the First World War. He was revered by many military men in the United States. It was generally known that General Pershing had maintained a close friendship with him since 1918. There were very few indeed in Washington who had ever heard of Marshal Foch's comment upon his colleague: "If the job requires that nothing be done, Pétain is your man." There were very few who were familiar with the devious part that Marshal Pétain had played in French politics behind the scenes for more than two decades, or who knew of his conviction that France could regain her earlier dominant position in Europe only if the French Republic were replaced by a monarchy or some form of dictatorship.

No one in Washington had as yet had the opportunity of hearing what was later revealed by Alexis Léger, for many years the brilliant Secretary General of the French Foreign Office: as far back as 1935, when Marshal Pétain and Pierre Laval had met at Warsaw as ambassadors at the funeral of Marshal Pilsudski of Poland, they had agreed, if later conditions favored their ambitions, to work together to establish in France the kind of authoritarian regime in which they both believed.

In the State Department the popular concept of Pétain as the rugged saviour of Verdun, and as an unselfish patriot devoid of all political ambition, had been modified by the reports sent by the American Embassy in Madrid where the Marshal had served as French Ambassador before the war. These showed him to be an excessively garrulous and vain old man chiefly concerned lest the honors accorded him by the Franco Government might fail to measure up to what he regarded as his due. While it was felt that the Marshal's advanced age of eighty-five would make it difficult for him to act with the vigor and determination that the interests of France so imperatively demanded, there was at first little suspicion of his ultimate aim, and only some slight realization of the extent of Laval's influence upon him.

In appraising the Roosevelt Administration's policy toward France and the validity of the initial assumptions and objectives responsible for that policy, it is necessary to recall what took place between the armistice with Germany and the appointment of an American Ambassador to Vichy.

The hostility of the French people toward Britain, already acute as a result of Britain's failure to give France more armed help in the final weeks before her collapse, had grown still more bitter after Britain attacked the French warships at Mers el Kebir to prevent them from getting into German hands. One thousand French lives were lost in this engagement. Almost every shade of public opinion within France backed Pétain's severance of diplomatic relations with Great Britain.

General de Gaulle had gone to London at the time of the armistice to organize resistance in metropolitan France and in the French colonies. He had not yet been recognized by the British Government as head of a "government in exile." He had, however, been granted recognition as "leader of all free Frenchmen wherever they may be who rally to him in support of the Allied cause." But General de Gaulle was little known in France outside purely military circles. Prime Minister Reynaud had appointed him Under Secretary of State for War in the spring of 1940. Only a mere handful of junior French officers rallied to his cause. No political leaders of any standing were originally included in his "Free French" committee. While the American Government necessarily sympathized with de Gaulle's stand, it could not as yet consider recognizing officially his right to speak for the French people as a whole.

Hitler's all-out air assault upon England commenced early in August. By the middle of September the British had shown the Nazi Government that they could not be crushed by air attacks alone or cowed into a plea for peace.

Toward the end of September Churchill encouraged de Gaulle, with the support of the British Navy, to attack Dakar. The engagement resulted in total failure, not only because several French warships under Vichy's orders helped to repel the attack, but more particularly because of de Gaulle's mistaken belief that the local garrison and officials would support him if he appeared upon the scene. The venture further embittered

Franco-British relations and gave rise to the suspicion among the French—a suspicion carefully nurtured by German propagandists —that Britain intended to take for herself any parts of the French Empire upon which she could lay her hands.

In the early autumn Marshal Pétain appointed Pierre Laval Foreign Minister. Laval promptly made it plain that his policy would be one of supine collaboration with Hitler.

Pierre Laval has now paid the supreme penalty. Innumerable estimates of his personality and of his career have been published in recent years. I need attempt no new evaluation of that sinister and uneasy spirit. It is sufficient to say that when Pétain named Laval Minister for Foreign Affairs we knew that the English-speaking powers were now opposed by a man who was able, ruthless and wholly unscrupulous, and obsessed with as burning a hatred for England as was his colleague, Admiral Darlan, the guiding spirit of the French Navy.

No sooner had Laval come to the French Foreign Office than he made, without Pétain's knowledge, secret overtures to the Nazis. At the end of October he was given the opportunity of talking with Hitler. These preliminary discussions proved to be only a part of a tripartite negotiation. For the Nazi failure to crush Britain had convinced Hitler that he must now either persuade or force the Vichy Government into a policy of total collaboration against England, and simultaneously bring Franco in on his side. Only in that way could he gain control of Gibraltar and of North Africa and close the Mediterranean to British ships.

But when he met Franco after he had seen Laval he was presented with a series of Spanish demands to which he refused to agree. Not only did Franco insist upon getting huge quantities of food and armaments, which the Germans were even then ill-prepared to supply, but he demanded as a permanent part of the Spanish Empire Gibraltar, all Morocco and part of Algeria, besides additional territory in western Africa. The chief reason Hitler was unwilling to pay such a price for Spain's support was his fear that the knowledge of the agreement in France and North Africa would cause popular uprisings of which the British would take prompt advantage. The meeting between Franco and Hitler, therefore, had no practical results.

We can gauge from Hitler's sour outburst to Mussolini a few weeks later how far advanced were his preparations to occupy Spain, seize Gibraltar and dominate French North Africa. He wrote:

> Profoundly troubled by the situation, which Franco thinks has deteriorated, Spain has refused to collaborate with the Axis powers. I fear that Franco may be about to make the biggest mistake of his life. . . . I deplore all this for from our side we had completed all our preparations for crossing the Spanish frontier on January 10 and to attack Gibraltar the beginning of February. I think success would have been relatively rapid. The troops picked for this operation have been especially chosen and trained. The moment that the Straits of Gibraltar fell into our hands the danger of a French change-over in North and West Africa would be definitely eliminated. I am, therefore, very saddened by this decision of Franco. . . . I still have the hope, the slight hope, that he will realize at the last minute the catastrophic consequences of his conduct, and that even tardily he will find his way to this battlefront, where our victory will decide his own destiny.

Laval, again without Pétain's knowledge, had assured Hitler that the Marshal would meet him after his conference with Franco. Pétain, although reluctantly, finally complied. The meeting took place at Montoire on October 24, and a secret written agreement was made.

Pétain was given the vague assurance that in "the new Europe" the Fuehrer would see to it that France occupied "the place to which she is entitled," and an equally vague assurance that, *if questions of detail could be settled*, France would be permitted "to employ certain contingents" beyond the stipulations of the armistice convention, "in order that she might take military measures in Africa." In return, Pétain permitted himself to be bamboozled into signing a declaration which stated that "the Axis powers and France have an identical interest in seeing the defeat of England accomplished as soon as possible."

In Washington we knew only that the Montoire meeting had taken place. Not until later did we have precise knowledge of the terms of the agreement. We feared the worst. The supreme question was the security of the French fleet. The reports from France insisted that Hitler had guaranteed Pétain final peace terms even more lenient than those foreshadowed by the armistice, provided the French Navy were at once transferred to Germany and provided Germany and Italy were granted French naval and air bases in northern and western Africa.

The President acted immediately. On the day following the Montoire meeting he sent a personal message to Marshal Pétain couched in these terms:

The government of the United States received from the Pétain Government during the first days it held office the most solemn assurances that the French fleet would not be surrendered. If the French Government now permits the Germans to use the French fleet in hostile operations against the British fleet, such action would constitute a flagrant and deliberate breach of faith with the United States Government.

Any agreement entered into between France and Germany which partook of the character above mentioned would most definitely wreck the traditional friendship between the French and American peoples, would permanently remove any chance that this Government would be disposed to give any assistance to the French people in their distress, and would create a wave of bitter indignation against France on the part of American public opinion.

If France pursued such a policy as that above outlined, the United States could make no effort when the appropriate time came to exercise its influence to ensure to France the retention of her overseas possessions.

Now that most of the secret state documents of that period have come to light it cannot be questioned that Laval had succeeded temporarily in deluding Pétain into the belief that France's best interests demanded a policy of collaboration with Germany. At no time was Pétain an Anglophobe of the Laval and Darlan variety. But he was at first entirely convinced—even though the British to his surprise had so far withstood the German assault—that England could not hold out for long; and that, if France did not take advantage of the opportunity now offered her, the peace terms that Great Britain might later secure would be at France's expense.

A few days after his receipt of the President's message the Marshal summoned Freeman Matthews, the American chargé d'affaires in Vichy, and made this statement to him:

To answer the anxiety of President Roosevelt, Marshal Pétain desires to state that the French Government has always preserved its liberty of action and that he (Roosevelt) knew that he might be surprised at an appraisement as inaccurate as it is unjust. The French

Government has declared that the French fleet would never be surrendered and nothing can justify questioning today that solemn undertaking.

Categorical as this assurance was, the situation still seemed so precarious to Mr. Churchill and to the President that Washington sent additional messages almost weekly. President Roosevelt suggested that the United States would buy France's two largest battleships, which were then stationed in North African ports. Even though Marshal Pétain refused to consider the proposal, the President sent word that the offer would remain open should the Vichy Government later change its mind.

All these crowded events took place during the late summer and autumn of 1940. By the beginning of November, the President was convinced that, if our Embassy in Vichy was to serve the purpose for which it was maintained, the time had come when he must appoint an Ambassador of the right caliber, who would be able to see Marshal Pétain whenever he desired, and who would be qualified to exert a decisive personal influence upon him.

In *Our Vichy Gamble* Professor Langer says[1]: "At the outset there was some thought of following the British example and at least allowing relations with the new France to lapse." I have no recollection that at any time during the summer or autumn of 1940 the President or the State Department had any serious thought that relations with the Vichy Government should be "allowed to lapse." There was, however, some discussion of two alternative courses: the first, to permit the American Embassy in Vichy to remain without an Ambassador in order to indicate

[1] Langer, William L., *Our Vichy Gamble* (New York: Alfred A. Knopf, Inc., 1947), p. 76.

our antipathy to the policies and personalities of the Vichy Government; and the other, to send with all speed an Ambassador of the kind most likely to prove effective.

It seemed to us that Marshal Pétain would probably be favorably impressed by the appointment of a very high-ranking officer of the American armed services. The personality and rank of such a man would inspire confidence, his military experience and background would make it easier for him to convince the Marshal that the British were not in such desperate straits as he had been led to believe, and he would be able to show the Marshal that the ability of the United States to prepare herself for defense and to help the British war effort was far greater than he had been told.

The President asked me to come over to his office in the White House late one November afternoon to discuss the pros and cons of several ambassadorial possibilities. Because of his association with Pétain in the First World War and their subsequent close friendship, General Pershing was considered first. But this idea had to be abandoned. The General was confined most of the time to Walter Reed Hospital and in no physical or mental condition to undertake the arduous duties involved. Several other prominent military figures were discussed, but those still in active service could not be spared and those who had been retired were discarded for one reason or another.

When I left him the President suggested that we each try to think of additional names and that I come in the following morning while he was breakfasting to talk the matter over further.

As I was driving into town the next day to keep my appointment at the White House, the name of Admiral William D. Leahy suddenly occurred to me. I had seen a good deal of Admiral Leahy during the preceding years when he was serving as Chief of Naval Operations, and had been associated with him in many White House conferences. The President, who had the utmost regard for him as a close friend and as a man of exceptional character, wide knowledge and incisive mind, had, upon his retirement for age, appointed him Governor of Puerto Rico. The Admiral had only recently entered upon his new duties. In view of the very serious problems that existed in Puerto Rico I was by no means certain that the President would feel justified in asking him to leave San Juan.

When I was shown into the President's bedroom I found him eating his usual hearty breakfast of grapefruit, coffee, cereal and eggs. He was sitting up in bed with a brown knitted sweater pulled over his pajamas. The morning was gray and raw, and as an added protection his blue navy cloak was thrown around his shoulders. Over the bedspread were scattered the *New York Times* and the *Herald Tribune*, and the Washington *Post*, which constituted his early morning reading.

"Have you any ideas," he asked.

When I suggested Admiral Leahy, the President's face immediately lit up as it always did when a new idea appealed to him. Without further ado he seized the telephone at his bedside and asked the operator to get the Admiral on the long-distance telephone. For some reason the circuits could not be cleared and the following message was, therefore, sent in naval code:

We are confronting an increasingly serious situation in France because of the possibility that one element of the present French Government may persuade Marshal Pétain to enter into agreements with Germany which will facilitate the efforts of the Axis powers against Great Britain.

There is even the possibility that France may actually engage in war against Great Britain and in particular, that the French fleet may be utilized under the control of Germany.

We need in France at this time an Ambassador who can gain the confidence of Marshal Pétain, who at the present moment is the one powerful element of the French Government who is standing firm against selling out to Germany.

I feel that you are the best man available for this mission. You can talk to Marshal Pétain in language which he would understand.

And the position which you have held in our own Navy would undoubtedly give you great influence with the higher officers of the French Navy who are openly hostile to Great Britain.

I hope, therefore, that you will accept the mission to France and be prepared to leave at the earliest possible date.

Admiral Leahy's acceptance was immediate. But since some time had necessarily to pass before he could wind up his affairs in Puerto Rico, he was not able to embark until early January.

Because the instructions given him by the President so clearly demonstrate the basic reasons for the Vichy policy, these excerpts from them are worth quoting here:

I desire that you endeavor to cultivate as close relations with Marshal Pétain as may be possible. . . . You should stress our firm conviction that only by defeat of the powers now controlling the destiny of Germany and of Italy can the world live in liberty, peace and prosperity; that civilization cannot progress with a return to totalitarianism. . . . I believe that the maintenance of the French fleet free of German control is not only of prime importance to the defense of this Hemisphere but is also vital to the preservation of the French empire and the eventual restoration of French independence and autonomy. . . . It has been a cardinal principle of this Administration to assure that the French fleet would not fall into German hands and was not used in the furtherance of German aims. . . . You will undoubtedly associate with high officers of the French Navy. I desire, therefore, that, in your relations with such officers, as well as in your conversations with French officials, you endeavor to convince them that to permit the use of the French fleet or naval bases by Germany or to attain German aims, would most certainly forfeit the friendship and good will of the United States, and result in the destruction of the French fleet to the irreparable injury of France.

Admiral Leahy was to insist that the French warships then in Martinique be immobilized. He was, however, instructed to state categorically that as far as the French colonies in the Western Hemisphere were concerned, all that the United States desired was the maintenance of the *status quo.*

On the positive side he could assure Marshal Pétain that the United States would help the Vichy Government to improve economic conditions in French North Africa. Further, through the American Red Cross we would send food to France, particularly for the children, provided this assistance would not impair Britain's military position.

By the time Admiral Leahy reached his new post, the anomalies of British policy had already begun to create difficulties for us in carrying out our own Vichy policy. It will be remembered that Pétain had severed diplomatic relations with England after the attack at Mers el Kebir. The British blockade of metropolitan France and of French African ports was generally effective. Consequently, no American shipments to French ports could be made without a British navicert. Any American economic assistance to France was, therefore, contingent upon British approval.

Mr. Churchill has written in the second of his volumes on the Second World War,[2]

I was glad when at the end of the year (1940) the United States

[2] Churchill, Winston, *Their Finest Hour* (Boston: Houghton Mifflin Co., 1949), p. 508.

sent an Ambassador to Vichy of so much influence and character as Admiral Leahy, who was himself so close to the President. I repeatedly encouraged Mr. MacKenzie King to keep his representative, the skillful and accomplished Mr. Dupuy, at Vichy. *Here at least was a window upon a courtyard to which we had no other access.*

We, of course, needed to keep that window open in our own interest. But quite apart from that, it seemed to us in Washington that the very fact that we immediately informed the British Government of everything we learned through that window should have persuaded Mr. Churchill and the members of his Government that we might well be considered capable of deciding how the window had best be kept open. Unfortunately, they did not feel that way.

Officially, Mr. Churchill supported the American policy. Both his records and those of President Roosevelt will show how very frequently the British Prime Minister sought, and successfully, to have the President employ his diplomatic relations with Vichy to prevent Marshal Pétain from sanctioning measures that might well have proved disastrously damaging to the British military position.

Mr. Churchill further says in the volume from which I have just quoted, "Our consistent policy was to make the Vichy Government and its members feel that, so far as we were concerned, it was never too late to mend."

The British Government even went so far as to hold conversations with a personal representative of Marshal Pétain. At the time of the Montoire Conference King George sent a personal message to the Marshal. At the same time, it is true, British representatives were seeking repeatedly—without success—to induce General Weygand, as soon as Pétain named him supreme French

Commander in North Africa, to throw off his allegiance to the Marshal and to come in on the Allied side.

We by no means failed to recognize Mr. Churchill's difficulties with General de Gaulle. Ensconced in London with his committee, General de Gaulle bitterly resented any direct or indirect approach by the British Government to the authorities of Vichy. He demanded that all questions relating to France be submitted exclusively to him. As Mr. Churchill so aptly says, "He had to be rude to the British to prove to French eyes that he was not a British puppet. He certainly carried out this policy with perseverance."

We could understand that the British were righteously indignant at the role played by the Vichy regime; we conceded the logic of their desire to build up de Gaulle so that he would be more likely to gain the adherence of France's possessions overseas. Still it was often highly difficult for us to understand how Mr. Churchill himself could urge us to stretch our diplomatic influence in Vichy to the fullest possible extent in Britain's behalf, while at the same time agencies of the British Government, over which he possessed full authority, used every propaganda weapon at their command to convince both the British and the American people that our Vichy policy was one of contemptible appeasement, and that in Britain's best interest we should withdraw our Ambassador and sever all relations with the regime.

I believe this extraordinary paradox resulted from the fact that many men of high authority in the British Information Service, and in British Intelligence as well, made use of their positions to further their own frequently almost fanatical Free French views rather than the policies to which their Government appeared to be so definitely committed. Certainly our own record is not devoid of similar instances where high-ranking officials have pursued their own individual foreign policies rather than the policy officially laid down by the Government.

We knew that many of the lesser officials in the British Foreign Office were so captivated by the Free French Committee that they lost no opportunity to discredit the maintenance of diplomatic relations between Washington and Vichy. We knew also that influential figures in other departments of the British Government were still more vehement. We knew that many prominent American editors and columnists were constantly being incited by their British friends of this ilk to attack American policy, and to try to persuade the American people that their Government should immediately abandon all relations with Vichy in order to deal exclusively with de Gaulle and his Free French Committee in London.

The difficulties that the State Department faced in coping with the French situation were in all conscience serious enough without having at the same time to deal with a backfire at home sedulously kept ablaze by agents of a Government whose war effort we were doing our utmost to assist. The task was made no easier by the fact that the highest British authorities with whom the President and the State Department dealt, Mr. Churchill, the Prime Minister; Mr. Eden, the Foreign Secretary; and Lord Halifax, the British Ambassador in Washington, were nine times out of ten wholly unaware of what was going on, and very naturally inclined to deny with considerable asperity the accuracy of any charges brought against their subordinates.

I recall very well indeed an instance which, although unrelated to our policy toward France, illustrates rather startlingly the recurrent failure of the British Government's right hand to know what its left hand was doing.

After the German occupation of Denmark an arrangement had been made by which the British Government was to use the Danish Merchant Marine until the end of the war. Several of these Danish vessels had been sent to the port of Baltimore. When the ships were due to sail it was learned that a considerable number of Danish seamen were not to be found. They were scattered throughout the numerous taverns on Baltimore's waterfront. Thereupon some zealous officials of the British Intelligence hired a quantity of trucks, manned them with the necessary number of British naval shore police and, with a blithe disregard for the local American authorities, proceeded from bar to bar and by main force dumped all the alleged Danish deserters they could find into the trucks for return to their ships. When the municipal authorities in Baltimore heard of this they promptly telephoned to me. I as promptly notified the British Ambassador. Lord Halifax, needless to say, had received no news of the occurrence, let alone any intimation that such action was to be taken. He was aghast at the reaction that might be provoked, even in wartime, if the American public learned of so flagrant a violation of American sovereignty, and one so painfully reminiscent of the British impressments of colonial days.

This was merely one of innumerable instances where there was no effective co-ordination between the many British agencies and services operating within the United States, and where the highest British authority here, namely, the Embassy in Washington, was given no chance to veto activities it would wholly have disapproved of, or that ran wholly counter to the policies decided on by the British Cabinet.

It must be said quite frankly that the objectives sought by Washington through its Vichy policy were attained in spite of, rather than because of, London.

Just before Admiral Leahy's arrival in Vichy, a sudden and dramatic change took place in the French Cabinet, which for the moment seemed to justify some slight feeling of optimism in Washington. Marshal Pétain, convinced after the Montoire Conference that Laval was maneuvering, with the support of Hitler's agents in France, to reduce him to the role of a figurehead, suddenly dismissed him and placed him under arrest. After extreme German pressure Laval was released. But Marshal Pétain stubbornly refused to reappoint him to any office. He replaced him as Foreign Minister with Pierre Étienne Flandin and at the same time promoted Admiral Darlan to be Vice Premier.

Superficially the situation seemed to have improved. The arch prophet of collaboration had been relegated to German-occupied Paris. Marshal Pétain seemed to have shown that there was a limit even to his truck with the Germans.

Darlan, long known in France as the most political of all admirals, was violently anti-British, but he could not properly be called pro-German in the sense that Laval was pro-German. Flandin had been Foreign Minister in 1936 when France and England decided not to lift a finger to prevent Hitler's march into the Rhineland, a decision which we now know made the Second World War inevitable. He had been a prominent leader of the appeasement forces in 1939. But it could not justly be said that he was anti-British. Rather, as a convert to the thesis that Britain's day was done, he believed that the future safety of France depended upon inducing Germany to let France collaborate in the creation of a Nazi Europe.

But notwithstanding these modifications in the regime, it was a sorry spectacle that greeted Admiral Leahy upon his arrival in Vichy in the early days of 1941.

As we had hoped, he at once succeeded in establishing a close relationship with Marshal Pétain. The Marshal gave him renewed and specific assurance that he would do everything within his power not to go beyond the terms of the armistice with Germany. But in his first report Admiral Leahy said bluntly that, while many officials in the Vichy Government hoped for a British victory, they believed that a British defeat was inevitable; and that consequently "almost any compromise with Berlin" might be anticipated. The Ambassador added that while Marshal Pétain now had an intense dislike for Laval, he would probably take him back into his Cabinet under German pressure, notwithstanding his references to him as a "bad Frenchman."

Given Admiral Leahy's character, he was not likely to confine himself solely to analyses of the current situation or to the mere transmission to Washington of the rumors with which Vichy was replete. He set himself immediately to find new ways to enhance American influence and fortify the French will to resist. From the outset he urged that, in addition to the medical supplies and the milk for French children which President Roosevelt had agreed the American Red Cross should send in American vessels to unoccupied France, food and clothing in large quantities should also be supplied, so that the Pétain Government would not be faced with a condition of popular misery which the Germans might readily make capital of. He wished also to have the French people learn in this concrete way of the sympathy felt for them by the American people. In addition, he realized clearly how urgent it was that the United States should grant economic

assistance to French North Africa. It was the only way to forestall widespread unrest among the native population, with a consequent breakdown in French authority. That would be exactly
the pretext the Germans and Italians wanted for demanding that
the administration of the French African possessions be turned
over to them.

A month earlier the State Department had sent Robert
Murphy to North Africa to make a survey of the situation, and
to find out what steps we might take to supply North Africa's
economic needs. Mr. Murphy had long served with much ability
as Consul General and as Counselor of Embassy in Paris, and his
survey was undertaken with the full support and enthusiastic
approval of General Weygand and his fellow officials. It showed
that, if British navicerts could be secured, a highly desirable deal
could be arranged whereby French funds held in the United
States could be unblocked sufficiently to enable French North
Africa to secure the tea, sugar, and petroleum needed by the
native population, besides the other products that were required
if a total collapse of the economic system were to be prevented.

The arrangement we were thinking of was, however, delayed
for many weeks by the not unnatural determination of the
British to make sure that any deal we made would not help the
Nazis. In March an agreement was finally concluded. The
United States was to supply French North Africa with the products needed, upon the specific understanding that they all would
be consumed within North Africa. An even more important condition was that the French authorities should permit the dispatch
to North Africa of a number of American officials who would
have exclusive control in the ports and on the railways of all shipments coming from America. It was these same officials, of course,

who later proved invaluable in securing the information and in forming the local contacts without which the invasion of North Africa in 1942 could scarcely have succeeded.

From the start until the end of his mission, Admiral Leahy never lost sight of the cardinal fact that if the United States were to succeed in her diplomatic holding operation, her Ambassador could not be limited to the use of cajolery or threats in his dealings with Pétain and the Vichy Government. As early as January 16, 1941, he wrote to me in a personal letter: "If we wish to retain the confidence of the French people through the approaching critical period of food and fuel shortage, it is necessary for us to do something more than talk."

The Ambassador was convinced that America could send unoccupied France supplies of relief clothing, food and oils in such a way as to make it impossible for them to be of any service to the Germans. These supplies would show the French people in the unoccupied zone that their friends across the Atlantic were enabling them to be spared the suffering of their compatriots under German control.

Here again, however, and for the same reason we ran headlong into British opposition.

To offset the effect American relief might have on French public opinion, the Germans in the spring of the same year authorized the release of 200,000 tons of wheat from northern France for use in the unoccupied zone. At about the same time Darlan authorized the issuance of a boastful statement declaring that, if the British attempted to block the Vichy Government's efforts to bring food from northern Africa to prevent "starvation" in unoccupied France, the French Navy would sink any British vessel that attempted to interfere.

In the end, while the British ultimately permitted American economic assistance to North Africa on a large scale, American relief to unoccupied France amounted to little more than Red Cross shipments of food, milk and clothing for children, and vitamins. Yet even these small contributions had a very marked effect upon French morale, and served beyond the shadow of a doubt to convince the French people that the United States would remain their friend if they would only hold firm as far as it was humanly possible. The growing American popularity in France was reflected in the statement Admiral Leahy reported Pétain made to him in April, "that America was the only friend now remaining to France, and the only hope for the future of his country and of his people."

The early spring and summer of 1941 were a desperately depressing time for all France, and particularly for those who still hoped for a final British victory. The British attempt to help Greece had ended in the disaster in Crete. The British efforts to check the onward march of the German and Italian armies through North Africa into Egypt seemed foredoomed to failure. French hostility toward Britain was again aroused by the seizure of Syria by British and Free French forces. Many French who prayed for American intervention in the war began to lose hope that the United States would ever take action; in their despair they were the more readily inclined to believe the German propaganda that the United States could not build up sufficient military power in time to prevent a total German victory.

The German attack upon the Soviet Union the end of June had but little effect in rallying French morale outside of the Communist centers. When we remember that there were hardly any high-ranking military officials in the United States who at that time believed that Russia would prove to be anything more than a pushover, and that most of them were even certain that the Russian armies would be hopelessly routed in less than three weeks, it is not surprising that the French saw little cause for hope in Hitler's egregious blunder.

Lend Lease and President Roosevelt's "Arsenal of democracy" speech in the spring, and his announcement in September that German and Italian vessels entering American waters did so at their own peril were very definitely shots in the arm to French public opinion. But their effect could by the very nature of things be only temporary to a people living under the constant shadow of fear.

Marshal Pétain and Darlan, who had now become the supreme authority in the Vichy Cabinet, were so shaken by the course of events that in July, with hardly a protest, they permitted Japan to take over control of Indo-China.

In the belief that it would distract public attention Pétain now had recourse to the project with which he had been so long obsessed. On August 12, in an address to the French nation that might well have been written for him by Goebbels, he announced the definite dissolution of parliamentary and democratic government, and proclaimed the creation of a "new France," of which he would ostensibly be the dictator, but in which it was all too clear he would be speaking only in his German masters' voice.

Pétain's action was proof, if proof were needed, of his increasing senility. It stimulated the will to resist of many elements in France that had until then been stunned or supine. French resistance for the first time became active. German retaliation in the form of the brutal assassination of French hostages did much to kindle a fire in the French soul which burned ever more steadily during the coming years.

Admiral Leahy believed that the most practical encouragement the United States could give the resistance movement, which was growing noticeably as the autumn months went by, was to speed up American economic assistance, especially since all indications pointed to a desperate food shortage in unoccupied France during the winter of 1942. He wrote to me as follows:

> Without any consideration whatever to the humanitarian aspect of providing relief, it would be advantageous to the cause of America to continue to hold the regard of the French people both in Africa and in continental France by the provision of necessities in limited amounts and under controlled distribution. . . . We have succeeded in making the French people and even some officials, including the Marshal, believe that the traditional amity between the two peoples is still maintained and that it is a matter of high interest to the people of America.

It was, of course, understood by all of us that, should Pétain and Darlan fall down on their promises to us, or actually collaborate with Germany in a way that impaired the British war effort, not only would shipments of supplies be immediately stopped, but our Ambassador himself would at once be recalled.

We now learned that the Germans were again pressing for bases in Tunisia and in Algeria. As the war had progressed General Weygand had gradually become convinced that a final German victory was by no means inevitable. While consistently refusing to agree to any specific measure that ran counter to Pétain's instructions, he tended more and more to facilitate

American activities in North Africa. He protested vigorously any decision by Vichy that would permit further German infiltration in the regions under his control, and opposed all German and Italian efforts to requisition French matériel in North Africa that would be of service to them in their Libyan campaign.

We now know that as early as the previous December, eleven months before, Hitler had insisted that Weygand be removed. In a letter he wrote to Mussolini on December 31, 1940, Hitler said:

> The French Government have dismissed Laval. The official reasons which have been communicated to me are false. I do not doubt for a moment that the real reason is that General Weygand is making demands for North Africa which amount to blackmail, and that the Vichy Government is not in a position to react without risking the loss of North Africa. I also consider it probable that there exists at Vichy itself a whole clique which approves of Weygand's policy, at least tacitly. I do not think that Pétain personally is disloyal. But one never knows.

At length Hitler determined that Pétain must comply with his repeated demands for Weygand's recall. On November 18 the Marshal at last gave in to a German ultimatum. To Admiral Leahy's insistence that he reconsider his decision, Pétain wearily replied, "I am a prisoner."

The Ambassador immediately recommended to the President that he be authorized to inform Pétain that, should the Vichy Government make any further concessions to the Nazis, he himself would be recalled to the United States. At the same time, and upon Admiral Leahy's urgent recommendation, the United States agreed to resume the program of economic assistance to North

Africa which had been halted by the news of Weygand's recall, provided the terms of the original agreement were confirmed in writing by the Vichy Government. This was promptly done.

Almost simultaneously came the attack upon Pearl Harbor. The United States now found itself involved in the World War.

So far North Africa had been kept out of German and Italian hands. In reply to a further and most urgent message from President Roosevelt, Marshal Pétain reaffirmed his oft-repeated assurance concerning the French Navy and French possessions in the Western Hemisphere, and insisted that his Government wished only to remain neutral and to refrain from breaking relations with the United States. He and Darlan emphasized, however, that they would be helpless in the face of a German ultimatum if it were backed by a threat to starve the French civilian population into submission.

Probably because the United States had entered the war, and Hitler was getting ever more deeply involved in Russia and in the Balkans, the situation in France and in North Africa for the moment remained relatively unchanged. In January, 1942, President Roosevelt tried through a confidential emissary to persuade General Weygand to return to North Africa and resume his command. The President assured him of full military and economic support from the United States. Weygand, however, consistently refused even to consider such a proposal.

The Roosevelt *démarche* became quickly known to the Germans. Soon thereafter most of the officials in North Africa who had been close to Weygand were summarily replaced with appointees of a collaborationist stripe. Pétain, in an interview with Leahy shortly thereafter, declared that he would not accept American military assistance in North Africa unless he himself should ask for it, and that, should the United States attempt to intervene on its own initiative, Vichy would resist by force.

By January, 1942, the situation with France had begun to deteriorate rapidly.

The trials at Riom of the former Prime Ministers Blum and Daladier had been ordered by Hitler in the hope that the testimony would arouse French public opinion against these eminent figures of the Third Republic. But the trials boomeranged and were suddenly halted by German behest. Nothing, as a matter of fact, could have proved to be more helpful in arousing the French heart and mind to the ignominy of France's present position than the magnificent defenses of French democracy made by the accused at that trial. It is not generally known that President Roosevelt sent a message to Pétain, when he learned that the trials were to take place, "demanding" that transcripts of the trials be furnished him.

The climax to the inevitable lessening of American influence at Vichy, once we were at war with Germany, came when Pétain submitted to the reappointment of Laval on April 18, as head of a new French Cabinet. This was the signal long since agreed upon in Washington, as Marshal Pétain well knew, for Admiral Leahy's recall from France. The Ambassador returned to the United States as soon as possible thereafter.

President Roosevelt's own judgment of the results of Admiral Leahy's mission had been expressed in a letter he had sent him early in April: "On the whole, I think our rather steady pressure has been successful to date."

As I myself had said to the British Ambassador in Washington at about the same time, "From the standpoint of the interests of both our Governments, what is desirable is to try and persuade the Marshal to play for time and to resist at every point with the hope that eventually the situation, in North Africa at least, can be stabilized and strengthened to our common advantage."

At least for eighteen months we had succeeded in that endeavor.

The story of our activities in France and North Africa and of our relations with the Vichy Government from the time Admiral Leahy left Vichy until November 8, when the American and British expeditionary forces landed on the shores of North Africa, is primarily a part of the military history of the Second World War. It may properly be regarded as the story of the outcome rather than as the story of the Vichy policy itself. It is a story that has been admirably presented, objectively and in full detail, in Professor Langer's *Our Vichy Gamble*.

This analysis of the Vichy policy and of President Roosevelt's part in deciding it and in carrying it out should not be concluded without a reference to certain purely personal equations that proved to have a greater effect upon events than could then have been anticipated.

The Vichy policy, as I have said, was frequently criticized by those very leaders of liberal public opinion in this country who constituted the President's most ardent personal supporters. At times President Roosevelt grew restive under the barrage. But he never wavered in his belief that the policy he was pursuing was the one best calculated to help the British in their war effort before Pearl Harbor, and afterward to promote our own diplomatic and military aims. Irritated as he might occasionally be by criticism that he thought factious, ignorant or unwarranted, he would soon brush the whole matter to one side and concentrate

upon more important issues. It was only actual disloyalty by those
to whom he had given his confidence that he never forgot.

Secretary Hull's reaction to criticism was wholly different. As
long as he was Secretary of State he regarded any public criticism of his department or of a policy for which he assumed responsibility as a personal affront, and an affront that he would
not forgive.

It must further be remembered—and Jim Farley's book, *Behind
the Ballots*, is the only book so far published that has thrown any
real light upon this exceedingly important factor in the President's later relations with his Secretary of State—that Franklin
Roosevelt's renomination in 1940 had aroused Mr. Hull's deep
and lasting resentment. Granted this fact, it was perhaps not
unnatural that the Secretary came to believe that the increasingly
sharp attacks upon the Department of State as the Vichy policy
was continued were instigated chiefly by the more liberal advisers
in the White House, with at least the tacit, if not open, approval
of the President himself.

I was confident then, as I am now, that there was not a shred
of justification for this assumption. Certainly the President did
not bare his breast and invite all the innumerable critics of the
Vichy policy to thrust at him rather than at his Secretary of State.
Nor was there any legitimate reason why, in a moment of growing international crisis, the President should serve as a lightning
rod to attract to himself all the criticism for an unpopular policy
for which he and his Secretary of State were jointly responsible,
and which both believed to be in the national interest, solely in
order that the Secretary of State might be spared public censure.
Yet hardly a week passed that Secretary Hull did not insist that

the President make some public statement in defense of the Vichy policy which would take the heat off the Department of State. It was incomprehensible to him, the President told me, that a man who had been prominent in active public life for more than thirty years could be so thin-skinned, particularly when no one in the Administration had had more favorable publicity in every part of the country.

The climax came when in December, 1941, the Free French forces of General de Gaulle seized the two small French islands of St. Pierre and Miquelon off the coast of Canada. As long as the powerful radio installation there remained in Vichy's hands, the British regarded it as a threat to the safety of Allied vessels in the North Atlantic. It undoubtedly was a danger. The problem was embarrassing to the United States since we had assured the Vichy Government that the *status quo* would be maintained in all France's possessions in the Western Hemisphere. The solution we had proposed—that the islands be placed under the supervision of Canada for the duration of the war, without, however, changing their status—was undoubtedly the wisest solution in view of all the circumstances. De Gaulle, however, seized the islands without the prior knowledge of either the British, Canadian, or American Governments. After the seizure had been accomplished with the apparent acquiescence of the inhabitants, Mr. Churchill, who was then visiting Washington, at first refused to agree that de Gaulle should be compelled to withdraw.

To forestall any violent reaction in Vichy, with the attendant possibility that Pétain might retaliate by suddenly granting the Nazis bases in North Africa, Mr. Hull decided at a State Department meeting on Christmas Day, at which I was present, to issue a public statement that would make it clear that de Gaulle's action had been taken without the prior knowledge or consent of the United States. The statement, which was drafted by Samuel Reber of the department, referred to de Gaulle and his committee as "the so-called Free French." The term "so-called" was, of course, exceedingly unfortunate, since it was subject to misinterpretation, and appeared—particularly to wishful thinkers—to convey the charge that the Free French Committee was misrepresenting its real character.

The statement created a violent uproar throughout the United States, Canada, and the United Kingdom. Every propagandist for the Free French cause seized it as a new and welcome means of attacking the Vichy policy. The Department of State was flooded with abusive and condemnatory messages. Mr. Hull, as usual, sought relief from the President. But for once the President refused to take any action. He thought the department's statement ill-advised, and he said so flatly. As Mr. Churchill writes[3] he "seemed to me to shrug his shoulders over the whole affair." The President's attitude caused Mr. Hull's smoldering resentment to reach white heat. As soon as I returned from the Rio de Janeiro Conference of Foreign Ministers a few weeks later, he betook himself to Florida whence for some time to come he even refused to speak with the President on the telephone. As he relates in his own version of this incident:

The refusal of the President to bring more pressure on Mr. Churchill to clarify the relations between Great Britain and the United States with regard to de Gaulle and Vichy was one of several

[3] Churchill, Winston, *The Grand Alliance* (Boston: Houghton Mifflin Co., 1950), p. 667.

factors that almost caused me to resign as Secretary of State in January, 1942. I so seriously considered resigning that I pencilled out a note to the President tendering my resignation.

Upon his return to Washington in the late spring, relations with the President were patched up and superficial cordiality reigned for some time to come. But the whole episode accentuated the fundamentally dissimilar characters of the two men chiefly responsible for the conduct of American foreign policy during the acutely critical days that were still to come, and sharply increased the President's disinclination to have more than official relations with his Secretary of State.

As Robert Sherwood has so accurately written,[4] "The episode was indeed, a flea bite, but it developed into a persistent, festering sore. It was a source of infection before D-Day in Normandy and after it."

In his book Professor Langer summarizes most aptly what the Vichy policy really was. He truly says:

It never was and never became a policy that we thought we could rely on. Quite the contrary, it was a day by day, hand to mouth policy all the way through. No one in the Department liked the Vichy regime or had any desire to appease it. We kept up the connection with Vichy simply because it provided us with valuable intelligence sources and because it was felt that American influence might prevail to the extent of deterring Darlan and his associates from selling out completely to the Germans.

Both in its execution and in its aftermath it was a policy that required decisions nearly every week at the top level from the late summer of 1940 until the invasion of North Africa in

[4] Sherwood, Robert, *Roosevelt and Hopkins* (New York: Harper & Brothers, 1950), p. 489.

November, 1942. Every single one of the important decisions was either made or personally approved by the President himself.

If President Roosevelt had been governed by his individual preferences, if he had been swept away by his emotions, or if he had given in to the constant pressure brought to bear upon him by the extreme New Dealers in his following, the Vichy policy would have been ended at an early date.

But if the President had not decided upon and persisted in that policy despite all the obstacles he encountered, it is my considered judgment that a wholly collaborationist Government, utterly subservient to the Nazi regime, would have been installed in Vichy early in 1941. Had that happened, Spain would in all probability have found it impossible to resist German pressure; the Mediterranean would have been closed to the British; the remainder of the French fleet would have passed into German hands; North Africa would speedily have come under German and Italian control; and the ultimate victory of the Western powers would have at the best been long postponed.

CHAPTER III

Far Eastern Policy before Pearl Harbor

EVEN the most friendly of the many Roosevelt biographers have a tendency to imply that the President gave little thought to foreign affairs before 1939. The impression created is far from accurate.

In the first place I doubt whether any American President since John Quincy Adams has been so well versed in the diplomatic history of his own country or so thoroughly familiar with the modern history of Europe or of Asia. His knowledge of geography was exceptional and his grasp of the principles of geopolitics almost instinctive.

During his first Administration the desperate condition of the country necessarily forced the President to dedicate the greater part of his attention to the reform and recovery program. Yet even during those first hectic "Hundred Days" of the New Deal there was hardly a major foreign government that did not send a spokesman to Washington to talk over its own problems, as well as world problems, with the President.

It is quite true that during Hitler's first years in power the President, like most of us, underestimated the extent of the Nazi menace. But he never underestimated the danger to the United States in the course of aggression on which Japan had embarked in 1931. In the four months between his first election and his inauguration he conferred twice with Henry L. Stimson, then Secretary of State under Hoover, on Far Eastern affairs. He soon thereafter announced that he was wholeheartedly determined to support the Stimson policy of nonrecognition of Japan's conquest of Manchuria.

Now generally forgotten apparently is the President's deep concern in the success of the disarmament conference held in 1933. In fact, about the only common-sense recommendation laid before the Conference was the Roosevelt proposal to define aggression.

As early as the winter of 1936 the President was already so worried by developments in Europe and Asia that he initiated the Inter-American Conference for the Maintenance of Peace, to insure the defense and solidarity of our hemisphere should it be confronted with a world war. One may also recall his initiative in creating the Intergovernmental Committee on Refugees in 1938, and his repeated efforts to dissuade Hitler and Mussolini from their fatal partnership in crime, as additional concrete evidence of his constant concern with foreign affairs.

Almost at the outset of his first term he ordered the Treasury Department to see what could be done to help Chiang Kai-shek's Government to overcome the ever increasing economic difficulties caused by the Japanese threat. Arming the Chinese forces and keeping them mobilized was a vast drain on China's resources. The Government was unable to secure adequate revenues. Worst of all, the shrinkage of Chinese currency was creating a chaotic situation even in the Chinese provinces that were in no immediate danger of Japanese invasion. Here the responsibility could not be laid at Japan's door. The problem was created by the Silver Purchase Act passed by the Congress of the United States in 1934. Silver had long been the basis for China's currency. When we increased the price of silver from thirty cents to $1.29 an ounce, it was not long before China's silver came flooding into the United States. In China the results were disastrous. Her business life was dislocated. Her export trade from the ports that were still open came to a halt. Inflation commenced the long upward spiral that reached such fatal heights by the time the Nationalist Government later took refuge at Chungking.

Unfortunately, all the help the President could offer were recurrent loans from various governmental agencies, and recurrent suggestions for internal reform. The loans were necessarily no more than stopgaps. The suggestions, whether well or ill considered, were scarcely feasible under the conditions then existing in the invaded country. The one sure method to prevent increasing chaos—the repeal of the Silver Purchase Act—was wholly impracticable, because of our own recovery program and because of the influence of the silver states in the Congress.

The preferential attention which the President gave at first to Far Eastern problems was partly due to purely personal reasons. As Assistant Secretary of the Navy for more than seven years, he had become imbued with the Navy's conviction that Japan was America's Number 1 antagonist. And no one close to the President could have failed to recognize the deep feeling of friendship for China that he had inherited from his mother's side of his family. His mother, in fact, had lived in China as a small girl, and he himself loved to tell over and over again stories of the dealings members of his family had had with various Chinese dignitaries and merchants in the earlier decades of the nineteenth century. A personal equation of this kind undeniably influences the thinking of a man even in high office. Quite apart from the moral, the international or economic issues that were involved, it was, therefore, only natural for the President to be profoundly concerned when Japan first invaded Manchuria. He became ever more incensed by Japan's conduct as the years passed.

In the spring of 1934 the Japanese Government issued a proclamation that in effect asserted its right to hold a protectorate over China. A few months later Japan announced her intention of withdrawing from the Washington Naval Treaty which limited the naval armaments of all the major powers. In 1936 Japan aligned herself with Nazi Germany and Fascist Italy by signing the Anti-Comintern Pact. In July of the following year the Japanese armies invaded China proper, beginning the ever expanding occupation of Chinese territory that was to continue uninterruptedly until Japan's final defeat eight years later.

It had by now become perfectly clear that all the liberal and Western-minded men who had once been real factors in Japan's political life had no longer any voice in determining Japanese policy; the ultranationalists and militarists had a firm grip upon the Government, and nothing short of force, or the conviction that they would encounter superior force, would make them abandon their plan to impose Japanese suzerainty over the whole of the Far East.

Neither China nor Japan had officially declared war upon the other. The President decided to take advantage of the discretion granted him by the Congress and refused to invoke the Neutrality Act which would have prevented the sale of munitions to both countries. Had the Act been applied, its effects upon China would have been far more harmful than its effects upon Japan; for China was already almost entirely dependent upon the United States for its means of self-defense.

What more could the United States do in the light of the conditions that then existed? Secretary Hull periodically issued pious remonstrances, but these, needless to say, proved as a deterrent to be as potent as the proverbial snowball in Hell. As Herbert Feis so truly says in his admirable book, *The Road to Pearl Harbor*, "We were trying to make foreign policy out of morality and neutrality alone."

France, confronted with a rearming Germany, was preoccupied with her own defense. The smaller countries with possessions in the Far East had no force at their disposal. The British Government, so long as Stanley Baldwin was Prime Minister and such men as Sir John Simon and Sir Samuel Hoare were Foreign Secretaries, refused to consider any kind of concerted international action. It had been largely responsible, as the Japanese aggression in Manchuria and Mussolini's invasion of Abyssinia so depressingly demonstrated, for preventing the League of Nations from imposing sanctions upon any powerful aggressor.

All through the summer of 1937 the President grew increasingly restive. He had become convinced that in her own interest the United States should not sit placidly by while a brutal military dictatorship allied with Nazi Germany and Fascist Italy moved to bring the immense resources and the power of China and of southeastern Asia under its own control. In any world in which such regimes became dominant, human freedom and democracy could not long survive.

Apart from issuing additional "preachments" Secretary Hull suggested no concrete action. Protests against the seizure of American properties and interference with American nationals in China were from time to time registered with the Japanese Government. But as the scope of the Japanese occupation of China grew, our protests were increasingly disregarded.

Finally, the President ordered the Navy to send him large-scale maps of the Pacific. These were placed upon a stand in his White House office. He had come to a conclusion about something that could perhaps be done.

It was in July, 1937, shortly after Japan's invasion of China, that he first talked over with me the plan that he had in mind. This was no less than to impose upon Japan a trade embargo to be enforced by units of the American and British Navies stationed at strategic points in the Pacific. Japan's economy depended largely upon the American and British markets. If these markets were denied to her, Japan could not hope for long to continue her onward march.

I remember asking the President whether he did not believe, since we were fully aware that the Japanese Army controlled the Cabinet of Prince Konoye, that such a step on our part must necessarily result in war. He said he did not think so. Japan was already so heavily committed in China that her economy was stretched to the breaking point. If her trade were shut off she would bog down long before she could get access to the oil and other raw materials in Southeast Asia that she would need. He did not believe she would dare risk war at that juncture.

I also remember asking him what assurance he had, in view of our past experience, that the British Government would be willing to go along with so radical a policy. His answer to this was that he had reason to hope that the new British Cabinet—for Neville Chamberlain had by now replaced Stanley Baldwin, and Anthony Eden was the new Secretary of State for Foreign Affairs—would not only have more "guts" than its predecessor, but that it might be able to see that the survival of the British Commonwealth was at stake. He added with a chuckle that the

British financial interests at least must realize that they would lose their vast commercial holdings in the Far East if Japan were permitted to make Asia a Japanese colony.

Shortly thereafter I left Washington for several weeks. During my absence the President abandoned his plan.

I know that Admiral Leahy, then Chief of Naval Operations, favored it. Whether the President was deterred by the remonstrances of the Secretary of State, by his knowledge that Mr. Chamberlain would not agree to joint action, by the opinion of most of the ranking admirals in the Navy Department that a quasi blockade of this character must end in war for which the American Navy was not then prepared, or by his realization that an isolationist Congress and an isolationist country would react violently against so radical a move, I never learned. I suspect, however, that he finally decided that public opinion would refuse to support any action that entailed even the remotest possibility of war.

Yet the incident is of peculiar interest since it lights up the background of the President's famous "quarantine" speech delivered in Chicago in October of the same year.

And what the President urged in that speech—that the decent members of international society "quarantine" all aggressor nations—was precisely what he had been turning over in his mind earlier that summer. The ostracism by any community of an evildoer implies that he will be cut off from all communication unless he is willing to reform. The free, decent and peaceful members of the family of nations had to decide, as the President put it, "whether our civilization is to be dragged into the tragic vortex of unending militarism punctuated by periodic wars, or whether we shall be able to maintain the ideal of peace, individuality, and civilization as the fabric of our lives."

On this issue he saw eye to eye with a man who was to become his Secretary of War three years later. On the day after the President spoke at Chicago, Mr. Stimson in a radio address made this categorical statement:

We have . . . gone far toward killing the influence of our country in the progress of the world. At the same time, instead of protecting, we have endangered, our own peace.

· Our recent neutrality legislation attempts to impose a dead level of neutral conduct on the part of our Government between right and wrong, between an aggressor and its victim, between a breaker of the law of nations and the nations who are endeavoring to uphold the law. It won't work. Such a policy of amoral drift by such a safe and powerful nation as our own will only set back the hands of progress. It will not save us from entanglement. It will even make entanglement more certain.

I have written elsewhere of the failure of most of the members of the President's own Cabinet to support his policy. Only Harold Ickes, Henry Morgenthau and Henry Wallace favored it. Mr. Hull was not only incensed that he had not been consulted, but was vehemently critical of the speech itself. A majority of the President's spokesmen in the Congress shared that feeling. Many Republican leaders took as much partisan advantage of the incident as they could, and, particularly in the Middle West, catered to isolationist sentiment by charging that the President was preparing to plunge the country into war.

The only way in which the country as a whole could have been persuaded to study the President's suggestions objectively was by the immediate delivery of a series of educational speeches throughout the country and over the radio by leading members of the Administration. So far as I can now remember not one of them volunteered.

In Mr. Stimson's book, *On Active Service*,[1] he accurately says, "In the months that followed Mr. Roosevelt seemed to conclude that the country was not ready for strong medicine, and the speech remained an isolated episode in a continuing pattern of inaction."

But President Roosevelt can hardly be held responsible for this "pattern of inaction." Had he been publicly supported by a few more men like Mr. Stimson himself, the American people might more easily have understood the gravity of the world situation and the fact that no greater threat to their peace or security could be found than in inaction itself.

Even in the armed services the feeling prevailed that anything that might touch off a showdown should be postponed. After the Japanese attack in Chinese waters upon the American gunboat *Panay*, it was only Admiral Leahy, so far as I now recall, who urged that the President's personal message to the Japanese Emperor, demanding a disavowal and indemnities, be followed up by the imposition of trade sanctions.

The President's dilemma was accentuated by the very natural reluctance of the other countries most directly affected by Japan's invasion of China to take any forthright action without the certainty of American co-operation.

The United States had suggested a meeting at Brussels, in November, 1937, of the nine signatories to the Washington Treaty of 1922, which regulated their relations in the Far East—

[1] Stimson, Henry L., *On Active Service in Peace and War* (New York: Harper & Brothers, 1948), p. 312.

Great Britain, France, Italy, the United States, China, Japan, the Netherlands, Belgium and Portugal. Although the Soviet Union was not an original signatory, she was invited to attend because of her vital interest in the Far East. Japan, however, refused to be represented, and spurned all idea of a negotiated solution of her aggression against China.

Norman Davis, so often our delegate at international conferences, was once more the American representative. Anthony Eden spoke for Britain. The other nations were represented by their leading statesmen.

After the failure to procure joint international action when Japan invaded Manchuria in 1931, or at the time of Mussolini's conquest of Abyssinia, it was hardly surprising that the Brussels conference opened in an atmosphere of defeatism or that it closed in an atmosphere of even deeper gloom. The only courageous note that was heard at the conference was sounded by Mr. Eden. But he made it emphatically clear that, if Britain were to join in imposing economic sanctions against Japan, the remaining signatories of the Nine Power Treaty must agree to join in collective military action to protect Britain's Far Eastern possessions should Japan decide to strike back. The Soviet Union and the Netherlands adopted the same attitude.

President Roosevelt thus found himself hemmed in within a vicious circle. The other powers, including the Soviet Union, were ostensibly prepared to undertake economic sanctions against Japan, but only if the United States would pledge itself to military action should this prove necessary. The President was willing to join in a commercial and financial quarantine of Japan, but he knew that neither the Congress nor American public opinion would authorize him to make any commitment that entailed the use of armed force were Japan to attack the Far Eastern possessions of some other power.

Upon his return to Washington, Norman Davis told me that he felt very keenly that he had not been properly supported by his own Government. Yet at that time, what more could the President have done? The "quarantine" speech had provoked a new wave of extreme isolationism in the United States. Only a few months before in the case of the Republican Government of Spain, Congress had almost unanimously adopted "neutrality legislation" which prevented the victim of an aggression from even securing armaments for defense from private manufacturers within the United States. Certainly it would reject a policy that might well involve this country in a war with Japan. It was a strange anomaly that the President who only twelve months earlier had been returned to office by the greatest electoral majority in the history of the United States should now find himself prevented from following the course upon which he believed the safety of the country depended.

All idea of a trade embargo upon Japan, whether unilateral or by joint international action, was now given up. Yet with the stubbornness that was so characteristic of him when he was convinced that he was right, the President continued to cast about for some other way to make it more difficult for Japan to continue her conquest of China. The possibilities were necessarily limited. One to which he gave considerable thought, and which he talked over with me upon several occasions, now seems far-fetched in the light of all that has subsequently taken place, but it was a prime favorite of the President for several months.

For a number of years large ocean-going Japanese fishing vessels, with canneries on board, had been extending their opera tions further and further into the waters adjacent to our own Pacific coast. An increasing number were cruising along the ocean shelf that extends some ninety miles from the coasts of the states of Washington and Oregon. The operators of the salmon fisheries of the Columbia River and other regions of our Northwest complained that the Japanese fishermen, although outside our own territorial waters, were taking the bulk of the salmon that were headed for American rivers and were thus depriving American fisheries of a large percentage of their normal catch.

The Japanese fishing fleets were reaping year by year a richer harvest. The President believed that, if their activities could be curtailed, Japan would be deprived of at least some percentage of her foreign exchange. He conceived the idea that the United States could legitimately maintain that conservation of the American people's normal food supply required that the ocean shelf extending from our Pacific coast be declared closed to all alien fishermen.

It was pointed out to the President that it would be inconsistent for the United States, at a moment when it was doing its utmost to promote the observance of international law throughout the world, to take action that would clearly violate principles that we ourselves had recognized. It was also argued that any such announcement would inevitably involve us in serious controversies with such maritime powers at Great Britain herself, and bring retaliatory action. At length, but most reluctantly, the President abandoned this project too.

It was always exhilarating to work with the President. He had an exceptionally fertile mind, and a mind which usually refused to concede that any problem was insoluble. He was unwilling to agree that in the realm of statesmanship there could be such a thing as a dead-end street. Mistakes he could and did make. But when we remember the number and magnitude of his problems, domestic and foreign, the wonder is that he was able successfully to solve so many of them. To me the ingenuity with which he so often devised the most effective solution in a given circumstance was a constant source of amazement.

During the next two years the President never swerved from his purpose to use such powers as the American people were willing to grant him to thwart Japan's undeclared war of conquest.

As the alignment of Germany and Japan became ever closer, it was evident to the President that the deal made by Stalin and Hitler in August, 1939, gravely increased the probability of an ultimate clash between Japan and the United States. For if at the instigation of the Nazis the traditional hostility between Russia and Japan was superseded by a full partnership in a joint conspiracy, the Japanese Army could no longer hope to expand in the north. It must, on the contrary, limit its ambitions to the south. But the more its ambitions there were realized, the greater would be the menace to the Philippines and to the legitimate strategic and commercial interests of the United States in the southern reaches of the Pacific.

How justified these apprehensions actually were has now been revealed by secret documents that have come to light since the end of the war. The fourth article of the so-called Ribbentrop Plan, the Nazi master-blueprint, provided that Germany, the Soviet Union, Japan and Italy would jointly agree to preserve as their respective spheres of interest:

a. the South Seas region for Japan;
b. Central Africa for Germany;
c. North Africa for Italy;
d. the Middle East, including Iran and India, for the Soviet Union.

And the official Japanese policy as secretly laid down by the Japanese Government in July, 1940, was declared to be:

1. to maintain a firm attitude toward America on the one hand; to effect on the other hand a sweeping readjustment of Japanese relations with the Soviet Union as well as a political combination with Germany and Italy; 2. to take stronger measures against French Indo-China, Hongkong and foreign concessions in China looking to the prevention of aid to the Chiang regime; 3. to practice more vigorous diplomacy toward the Netherlands East Indies, in order to acquire vital materials.

While, needless to say, neither the White House nor the Department of State had at that time any inkling of the precise details of these decisions, the new policies resulting from the rapprochement between Germany, the Soviet Union and Japan were plain for all who cared to see.

The professional Roosevelt critics and the fanatical Roosevelt-haters now, like some of the more liberal Roosevelt supporters then, make much of the fact that during the following critical years the American Government continued to permit the shipment to Japan of oil and of scrap iron and steel, all urgently needed in the prosecution of Japan's war effort.

In *The Road to Pearl Harbor* Herbert Feis has published a highly detailed and completely documented account of the successive steps that were taken between 1937 and the close of 1941 to restrict and eventually to cut off trade between

Japan and this country. But since I myself took some part in determining American policy at that time and bear my share of responsibility for the decisions reached, this additional explanation seems warranted.

The so-called "moral embargo" had been initiated by the Administration in June, 1938, to discourage private companies from shipping airplanes and airplane parts to Japan, and to dissuade American financial interests from extending credits to Japan. High octane aviation gas was subsequently included · in the moral embargo as well as all raw materials that could be used in the manufacture of airplanes.

The provisions of our Treaty of Commerce and Navigation with Japan prevented us from placing an embargo on exports to that country unless a similar embargo was imposed on exports to all other foreign countries. The treaty contained a six months termination clause. Consequently, only six months after notifying Japan of our intention to renounce the treaty could we shut off or restrict the oil and the scrap iron that she was buying in this market.

Moreover, the President, in view of the gathering storm in Europe, was seeking desperately to persuade the Congress to amend the Neutrality Act so that the Western democracies could procure here the means for self-defense. He feared the effect upon the country should Japan make an issue of the announcement that we intended to end the treaty. Yet on July 26, 1939, the notice of termination was given and this Government regained freedom of action in January of the following year.

In the summer of 1940, at the very moment when Hitler had subjugated France and when the fate of England seemed to be trembling in the balance, the Secretaries of War, of the Navy, and of the Treasury made a concerted effort to persuade the President to stop all exports of oil and of scrap to Japan. Their plan further provided that Britain's oil requirements were to be supplied by the Western Hemisphere, that the oil refineries and wells in the Netherlands East Indies were to be destroyed, and that the British were to concentrate upon the destruction of Germany's oil stocks and synthetic oil plants. They hoped in this way to halt the German and Japanese war machines.

As Mr. Stimson has recorded in his diary, I opposed their plan at a White House conference attended by Secretaries Stimson and Knox, and myself as Acting Secretary of State. I opposed it because I believed that in a moment of such supreme danger to the United States as the summer of 1940 it was unwise to risk goading an already berserk Japanese Army into an attack upon an almost crippled Britain and an almost defenseless Netherlands that would probably involve the United States herself in war. It seemed to me, especially in the light of Mr. Churchill's recurrent warnings, that a Japanese assault upon Britain's colonies in the Far East might be anticipated at any moment, and that it would be the height of imprudence for the United States to strike the spark that might readily set off the powder keg.

Moreover, both the Navy and the Army, as represented by Admiral Stark and by General Marshall, had expressed to me their insistent belief that such an embargo would most probably result in an early attack by Japan on the Netherlands East Indies and Malaya. The United States, they said, was not yet prepared for the war into which that action might draw her. I knew, therefore, that the views of the two Secretaries were not shared by the top-ranking professionals in their Departments.

The President was inclined to accept the recommendation of Stimson and Knox. He at first decided to sign a proclamation placing the export of all oil and of all scrap metals under control. But later, upon my most earnest appeal, he reversed his decision. The proclamation finally issued established controls only over lubricants that could be used in aviation and certain grades of scrap iron and steel.

The following year, after the Japanese armies had commenced their movement to the south, the control of the export of iron and steel scrap was made all inclusive by a further presidential order. The controls over the export of oil, however, remained unchanged for the time being.

With the signature of the Axis Pact in September, 1940, Japan openly became a full-fledged ally of Germany. The alliance was a patent attempt to intimidate the United States, and to prevent us from taking further coercive action against Japan and from giving further assistance to Great Britain. But by this time the dangers and uncertainties of the preceding months had been to some extent dissipated. The British had triumphantly withstood the German air assault. American military and industrial production was rising sharply. Our rearmament was proceeding apace. And both the American people and their Congress were far more disposed to see their government take resolute action.

Through intercepted messages sent out by the Japanese Government we knew in July, 1941, that Japan had decided to consolidate her stranglehold on French Indo-China, to take over Thailand, and to press still further southward.

The President instructed me to tell the British Government that

. . . if Japan now took any overt step through force or through the exercise of pressure to conquer or to acquire alien territories in the Far East, the Government of the United States would immediately impose various embargoes, both economic and financial, which measures have been under consideration for some time past.

He also instructed me to inform the Japanese Government that, if Japan moved into Indo-China, we could see no further use in continuing negotiations that Secretary Hull had begun the preceding winter in the hope that our common difficulties could yet be solved.

A few days later, on July 24, the Japanese invasion force arrived in Camranh Bay.

The President immediately sent for Admiral Nomura, the Japanese Ambassador. He requested Admiral Stark and myself, as Acting Secretary of State, to be present at the interview. He told the Ambassador that he had permitted the continued export of oil to Japan in the hope that this decision would tend to keep war out of the South Pacific. But, he added, if Japan now attempted to seize the oil supplies of the Netherlands East Indies, the Dutch would unquestionably resist, the British would immediately come to their assistance, and war would result between Japan, the British and the Dutch. In view of our policy of assisting Great Britain, the situation would immediately become exceedingly serious. The President concluded with this proposal which I quote from a memorandum of the conversation which I made at the time:

If the Japanese Government would refrain from occupying Indo-China with its military and naval force, or, if such steps actually had been commenced, if the Japanese Government would withdraw such forces, the President could assure the Japanese Government that he would do everything within his power to obtain from the Governments of China, Great Britain, the Netherlands and, of course, from that of the United States itself, a binding and solemn declaration, provided Japan would undertake the same commitment, to regard Indo-China as a neutralized country. . . . This would imply that none of the powers concerned would undertake any military action of aggression against Indo-China, and would refrain from the exercise of any military control within or over Indo-China.

As soon as it became apparent from the intercepted Japanese messages that Japan would persist in her venture, the President issued an executive order freezing all her assets in the United States, and thereby bringing under the direct control of this Government all financial and import and export trade transactions involving Japanese interests.

Both the British and Dutch Governments took similar action.

The phrase that Roosevelt once used in 1941, when he told Churchill that he was "babying Japan along," has been grossly misinterpreted to mean that his policy was one of feeble appeasement.

The concrete facts above cited, as well as even a cursory examination of the conditions that existed at the time the phrase was used, make it clear that no such interpretation is warranted. The "babying along" tactics were used after it was altogether clear that the Japanese militarists would never give up their plans for conquest unless they were met with superior armed force, and upon the urgent and repeated insistence of the Chief of Staff and of the Chief of Naval Operations that the United States must have time to prepare for defense. As the President wrote Secretary Ickes on July 1, 1941, when the latter insisted that a trade embargo be at once imposed upon Japan, they were adopted because "it is terribly important for the Control of the Atlantic for us to help keep peace in the Pacific. I simply have not got ENOUGH NAVY to go around."

During all these increasingly anxious months before Pearl Harbor the President was under constant pressure from those members of his Cabinet who were calling for a more vigorous policy. They contended that the risk of becoming involved in the Pacific when we were struggling to help Great Britain control the Atlantic and had as yet no two-ocean Navy was justified by the possibility that a more vigorous policy would cause Japan to abandon her plans for conquest.

There was at that time no one of my colleagues in the State Department who was less "appeasement-minded" than Herbert Feis, or who was more firmly convinced of the need for a positive and constructive foreign policy. His own conclusions, as published in his recent book,[2] are for that reason well worth quoting here:

My own best surmise is that stronger and earlier action would not have caused Japan to slow up, then desist from its course. More probably, I think, it would have caused it to move farther and faster. The Indochinese expedition would probably not have stopped in the north. The terms of the alliance with the Axis might well have been more clinching. Not improbably, Japan, despite the reluctance of its Navy, would have ceased to dally with the Indies. Or, in the coming January, when Hitler was greatly to want Japan to move against Singapore, it would have done so. In either event, the crisis in the Pacific might well have come during the winter of 1940-1941, instead of the next one.

[2] Feis, Herbert, *The Road to Pearl Harbor* (Princeton: Princeton University Press, 1950), p. 107.

Such, rather than peace in the Pacific, would have been, I think, the outcome of an earlier application of compelling sanctions, unless the United States had been willing (and sufficiently united in sentiment) at the same time to send the Pacific fleet to Singapore, to make known that it would join Britain, France and Holland in the defense of their Far Eastern possessions. That might have worked. If it did not, the United States would have been at war.

Throughout 1941 the Prime Minister had been urging the President to warn Japan that the United States would not stand to one side if she attacked Britain. The British position in Europe still seemed desperate at the beginning of 1941. Their navy, hard pressed to maintain the British lifeline across the Atlantic, could not have attempted to cope with the Japanese fleet in the Far East. The British Government was convinced that it was only fear of the United States that kept the Japanese from attacking the British colonies in the Far East that winter. Yet even as late as August, 1941, at the time of the Atlantic Charter meeting, the President did not comply with Mr. Churchill's insistent request that he issue a peremptory warning in the nature of an ultimatum to the Japanese Government "to halt and desist." He felt that, unless the Japanese Government were convinced that the threat would be at once backed up by superior force, it could only do more harm than good.

The story of Secretary Hull's negotiations, first with the Japanese Ambassador, Admiral Nomura, and ultimately with both Nomura and Kurusu, the special envoy sent by the Tojo Cabinet to Washington in November, 1941, has been recounted at length. Every incident, however trivial, in this final stage of our prewar relations with Japan was brought out under the full glare of publicity by the Congressional Pearl Harbor Investigating Committee. I am persuaded now, as I was then, that Secretary Hull's negotiations were fully justified.

In the course of the more than sixty conferences that took place between the Secretary of State and the Japanese representatives all means of reconciling fundamentally irreconcilable policies and interests were fully explored, in the attempt to avert, or at least to postpone, a final crisis—an effort on which both the United States Army and Navy ever more strongly insisted. This Government at last even considered offering the Japanese a *modus vivendi*, calling for a three month's truce, under the terms of which, in return for a Japanese agreement to refrain from all further aggression during that time, the American Government would relax its total embargo and freezing orders.

Before it was taken up with the Japanese envoys the proposal was submitted to several of the other governments most directly concerned, Great Britain, Canada, Australia and the Netherlands. They gave it only lukewarm approval, although no decided opposition. But when it was submitted to T. V. Soong, Chiang Kai-shek's brother-in-law, then serving as his special representative in Washington, and to Hu-Shih, the Chinese Ambassador, a tempest was aroused. They were both adamant in their insistence that, if the plan were carried out, it would amount to no more nor less than selling China down the river, and would irretrievably destroy whatever morale still existed among the Nationalist armies fighting the Japanese.

Unquestionably the mere fact that we were known to be willing to urge such a project, however justified, seriously impaired the confidence of Chiang Kai-shek and his entourage in the United States. It was indeed responsible for much of the friction and suspicion that clouded relations between Washington and the Nationalist Chinese Government in subsequent years.

T. V. Soong is, in my judgment, in many ways one of the ablest of the statesmen with whom I had to deal during the war years. He had made himself thoroughly familiar with the way in which public relations may most advantageously be handled in Washington and with the methods best calculated to enlist the sympathetic interest of influential members of Congress. In the course of his investigations he had learned that a former official who had recently taken up "the practice of law" in Washington could more than probably be of considerable help to him.

Owing to no small extent to the activities of this man, the day after the Chinese Embassy learned from Secretary Hull of the *modus vivendi* that was under consideration, the columns of many newspapers were filled with diatribes against the State Department, and with allegations that our "policy of appeasement" had now culminated in our being blackmailed by the Japanese. The corridors of the Senate and of the House of Representatives resounded with vehement protests. Chinese opposition was successful. The project was shelved. .

As we look back, it becomes entirely clear that in submitting such a project for the consideration of the Chinese Government we seriously weakened the moral strength of our position. It led the Chinese to suspect that the United States would be willing to sacrifice China if and when it served American interests. Most important of all, we can now see that Japanese agreement to the *modus vivendi* could have in no way averted the final catastrophe.

I do not believe that the President himself ever had any faith that the Hull negotiations would result in an agreement to which the American Government could legitimately subscribe. In my talks with him before the Atlantic Charter meeting as well as immediately thereafter—and this was at a time when the negotiations had reached a long impasse—he never gave me the impression that he thought any firm understanding with Japan was possible.

He did, however, make it very plain to me that he thought the immediate danger was an attack by Japan upon some British possession in the Far East, or even more probably upon the Netherlands East Indies. What worried him deeply was that, though this would immediately threaten our own vital interests, it might be impossible to persuade either the Congress or the American people that it was tantamount to an attack upon our own frontiers and justified military measures of self-defense. He felt, however, that Japan would not attack the United States directly until and unless we found ourselves involved in the European war.

In that connection these excerpts from a memorandum of Harry Hopkins written some weeks after Pearl Harbor and published in Robert Sherwood's *Roosevelt and Hopkins*[3] are of peculiar interest.

I recall talking to the President many times in the past year and it always disturbed him because he really thought that the tactics of the Japanese would be to avoid a conflict with us; that they would not attack either the Philippines or Hawaii, but would move on Thailand, French Indo-China, make further inroads on China itself, and possibly attack the Malay Straits. He also thought they would attack Russia at an opportune moment. This would have left the President with a very difficult problem of protecting our interests. . . .

[3] Sherwood, Robert, *Roosevelt and Hopkins* (New York: Harper & Brothers, 1948), pp. 428-429.

Apropos of the Roberts Report, which indicates that the State Department had given up all hope of coming to an agreement with Japan, it seems to me that hardly squares with the facts. It is true that Hull told the Secretaries of War and the Navy that he believed Japan might attack at any moment. On the other hand, up to the very last day, he undoubtedly had hopes something could be worked out at the last moment. Hull had always been willing to work out a deal with Japan. To be sure it was the kind of deal that Japan probably would not have accepted, but, on the other hand, it was also the type of a deal that would have made us very unpopular in the Far East.

Hull wanted peace above everything, because he had set his heart on making an adjustment with the Japanese and had worked on it night and day for weeks. There was no question that up until the last ten days prior to the outbreak of war he was in hopes that some adjustment could be worked out.

A further excerpt from an earlier part of the same Hopkins memorandum shows more clearly than any other contemporary document the difficulties in which the President was enmeshed in his persistent efforts to carry out the policy that he fervently believed was best calculated to promote the security of the United States.[4]

The President told me about several talks with Hull relative to the loopholes in our foreign policy in the Far East insofar as that concerned the circumstances in which the United States would go to war with Japan in the event of certain eventualities. All of Hull's negotiations, while in general terms indicating that we wished to protect our rights in the Far East, would never envisage the tough answer to the problem that would have to be faced if Japan attacked, for instance, either Singapore or the Netherlands East Indies. The President felt that it was a weakness in our policy that we could not be specific on

[4] *Ibid.*, p. 428.

that point. The President told me that he felt that an attack on the Netherlands East Indies should result in war with Japan and he told me that Hull always ducked that question.

I remember when I was in England in February, 1941, Eden, the Foreign Minister, asked me repeatedly what our country would do if Japan attacked Singapore or the Dutch, saying it was essential to their policy to know.

Of course, it was perfectly clear that neither the President nor Hull could give an adequate answer to the British on that point because the declaration of war is up to Congress, and the isolationists, and, indeed, a great part of the American people, would not be interested in a war in the Far East merely because Japan attacked the Dutch.

Harry Hopkins' remark that "the President felt it was a weakness in our policy" that we could not inform the British or the Dutch that we would join them in military action against Japan if their territories in Southeastern Asia were attacked is a remarkable understatement. The inability of the American President to say what he would do in certain contingencies was not merely a "weakness in our policy"; it had made it wholly impossible for him for a period of exactly four years to carry out the policy that he himself believed to be vitally important to our security.

In the light of the facts that I have recited the picture seems to me to be very plain. As early as the summer of 1937 the President had reached the positive conclusion that, if Japan were permitted to continue unchecked along the road upon which she had first set her feet in 1931 when she invaded Manchuria, world peace could not be maintained, and the security of the United States would inevitably be gravely jeopardized.

The "quarantine" speech of the following October failed to evoke any favorable congressional or popular response, but it did call forth a blast of furious denunciation which made it plain that the policy he believed to be essential could not be carried out. The Brussels Conference, which might have agreed upon joint collective action, failed for precisely the same reason. That kind of thinking still prevailed in the Congress and throughout the country up to and including the final days before Pearl Harbor.

There is surely good reason to believe that in 1937 a total trade embargo, imposed by a Britain not yet involved in a war for survival, together with the United States and the remaining members of the Nine Powers, and backed if necessary by force, could have compelled the Japanese Army to abandon its plans for aggressive expansion. But between 1939 and 1941 the imposition of such an embargo by a crippled Britain and a United States at bay, supported only by such scattered forces as the remnants of the Nine Powers could then muster, could have served only to incite Japan to risk an immediate war with the Western democracies.

The decision of the American people to reject the recommendation their President made to them in his "quarantine" speech lost this nation its best chance to avoid war with Japan.

America's need for a United Nations organization under which collective action against an aggressor might be instantly possible became more apparent to the President in consequence of his heartbreaking difficulties in finding ways to carry out a Far Eastern policy that would work. I know that he frequently recurred to this theme in our discussion of the drafts of what later became the United Nations Charter.

It is, of course, obvious that our Far Eastern policy during the first eight years of the Roosevelt Administration could not have been adopted unless the President had authorized the steps that were taken under it. In that sense, good or bad, successful or unsuccessful, Roosevelt must bear the responsibility for it. But it was never the policy that he himself would have adopted if he had been free to act as he wished. It was certainly not the policy upon which he had decided in 1937.

At this moment American forces, with overwhelming popular approval, are fighting in South Korea in compliance with the verdict of the United Nations that an aggression has been committed and that the members of the United Nations must join in collective action to repel the aggressor. It seems a far cry to that moment, thirteen years ago, when American public opinion was outraged at the mere thought that another aggressor, Japan, should be punished by a quarantine.

Yet is it not true that if that quarantine had been imposed in 1937, with Japan's knowledge that it would be supported by the armed might of all the countries that had signed the Nine Power Treaty, our troops would not presently be fighting in Korea? And would not China today be free of foreign domination, and able to join in an international attempt to bring into being a free, a peaceful and a prosperous Asia?

CHAPTER IV

The Decision that Saved New World Unity

THE flight seemed interminable that afternoon of January 12, 1942. We had taken off from Belem at dawn to cut across Brazil's bulge to Rio de Janeiro. The opaque green jungles of the Amazon Delta had long since given way to the more sparsely wooded ranches and farm lands that lie to the north of Bello Horizonte. Here and there the landscape was studded with white and purple mounds of Brunfelsia. The incredibly vivid colors of southern Brazil's early summer radiated from every hillside.

The plane rose and fell with metronomic monotony as we flew through the evenly spaced fat clouds with which the skies were dotted. For me at least reading had become impossible. Most of my fellow delegates to the coming Conference of American Foreign Ministers were seeking sleep as the surest refuge from the calamitous effects upon the inner man of the plane's attempt to ape an express elevator. In the rear compartment some of the newspaper correspondents were still deep in the poker game that had started soon after we left Miami. Mr. William Philip Simms was frowning over his notes. Mr. and Mrs. Drew Pearson were talking animatedly to Dr. Padilla, the Mexican Foreign Minister. Across the aisle Wayne Taylor and a group of American economists were sorting the mountains of memoranda they had brought along.

A radio message had just come in that thunderclouds hung heavy over Rio's harbor. Our landing would probably be delayed. Even at the best we would still have three hours. I began to rehearse once more every feature of the major problem which the Conference must face.

It was strange that so few Americans recognized how grave the crisis was. The damage done by the Japanese at Pearl Harbor had been kept secret for reasons of security. Axis strategy would have been greatly simplified had Japan's warlords known that our Pacific fleet was partially paralyzed. Yet, even so, the most casual newspaper reader should have realized that we had received a crippling blow and that the Pacific Coast from Canada to Chile was now exposed. It must be equally plain that the safety of the Panama Canal had suddenly become a matter of life and death and that the willingness of our neighbors to help us protect it and to co-operate in resisting further attacks against the hemisphere was of vital concern. The press and the radio were telling the public what the stakes were at the Rio meeting. But most Americans were assuming that this was going to be merely one more Pan-American conference—and why bore oneself by thinking about it?

I wished again, as I so often wished in those years, that national security permitted the public to be told the stark and uncensored truth.

The submarine menace compelled the greater part of the American Navy to stay in the Atlantic. Unless the British received the planes, munitions and food they needed they would be as desperately pressed as they were after France's collapse. Unless similar supplies could reach the Soviet Union through

Archangel and Iran the ability of the Red armies to keep on fighting would be problematical.

The South Atlantic had become one of the best hunting grounds of Axis submarines.

Chile, Peru and Ecuador were now open to Japanese invasion. Lower California was defenseless and largely unpopulated. The stretch from Mexico's Guatemalan frontier to northern Panama was equally vulnerable. Nazi agents swarmed through Central America. We knew that German "businessmen" and Japanese "farmers" had bought lands in Costa Rica and in Colombia only a few hundred miles from the Panama Canal. Germans had long been playing a leading part in running Colombia's domestic airlines. Italian Army aviators had trained Ecuador's air force. There were many thousands of Japanese in Northern Peru.

There was imminent danger to the safety of the United States in every one of these facts. Our Navy's traditional nightmare was a world situation in which it would have to fight a two-ocean war with a one-ocean fleet. That nightmare had now suddenly become a reality. Our only hope lay in having the uninterrupted use of the Panama Canal so that warships could at any given moment get from the Atlantic to the Pacific. Should the American republics fail to co-operate, the limited resources in ships and in planes that the United States then possessed might not be sufficient to insure their security. Should any American republic near the Panama Canal fail to take steps to control the activities of Axis nationals and their local followers, the Panama Canal might any day be bombed from the air or from the land and be blocked for many months. Secretary Stimson had told me just before I left that the radar and other instruments needed to make our Panama-based air patrols effective were as yet so few and so deficient that we could not be sure of being warned in sufficient time if the Japanese suddenly decided to attack the Canal in force.

Two other factors were almost equally disquieting.

A very great sector of public opinion in South America—especially in Army circles—had reached the conclusion that Hitler was invincible. It was thought that the help the United States could give Great Britain would be too little and too late to make it possible to defeat the Axis. This point of view not unnaturally was having its effect on several governments. It had already persuaded many of the more timorous statesmen that prudent neutrality was the wiser course.

The second factor was equally understandable. Chile, for example, had a coast of some 3,000 miles, lying at a great distance from the United States. If she were attacked, she could scarcely look for immediate help from us. Many leading politicians and journalists, even those most friendly to the United States and most anti-Axis in their own way of thinking, believed naturally enough that a break in relations with the Axis—and still more a declaration of war—would immediately bring retaliation which their Army and Navy could not withstand. The same conditions obtained in several other countries. It was only to be expected that every new Axis victory would strengthen these two schools of thought.

At the same time there were other factors that made me feel far more optimistic about the outcome of the Conference. The difference between our position in the hemisphere now and during the First World War was striking. In 1917 hatred of the United States had been widespread throughout Latin America. Sentiment favorable to Germany had then been so marked that only a few American republics had stood with the United States and the Allies. A far greater number had refused to modify their policy of strict neutrality.

All that had since been changed by the Good Neighbor Policy. The just resentment aroused by our armed interventions had been ended by our willingness to join in a convention forbidding all interference by one American republic in the affairs of another, and by the abrogation of all treaties giving the United States a right to intervene in other American countries. The Reciprocal Trade Agreements and the economic and financial co-operation we had offered our Latin-American neighbors had provided a practical and solid basis for the political solidarity which was steadily and rapidly growing. Feeling in Latin America toward the United States was friendlier than at any previous time in the history of the independence of the American peoples.

The proof was in the fact that later, after the attack on Pearl Harbor, the five Central American republics, together with Panama, Cuba, the Dominican Republic and Haiti, immediately declared war upon the Axis powers, and such great states as Mexico, Colombia and Venezuela broke all relations with them. In the southern republics, too, there was much popular support for the Western Allies.

However, South American affairs have for many generations been chiefly influenced by the relations between Argentina, Brazil and Chile, and several internal complications made it far from certain what the final position in those countries would be.

There is no more progressive or truly democratic member of the American family than Uruguay. After Pearl Harbor she wanted to take prompt action against the Axis. But Uruguay is a small country. Wedged in as she is between her two great neighbors, she would have found it exceedingly difficult to adopt this course if Argentina and Brazil both refused to.

The position of Bolivia and of Paraguay was similar. It was true that President Estigarribia—whose untimely death had tragically retarded Paraguay's recovery after the Chaco war—had freed his country from Argentina's grip. Paraguay had now swung over to a very intimate relationship with Brazil. But neither Paraguay nor Bolivia could be expected to adopt an international policy which differed from that of both Argentina and Brazil.

Peru and Ecuador were still engaged in the bloody controversy to which their century-old boundary dispute had suddenly given rise. This was taking up all their attention, and using up most of their resources. It was inconceivable, no matter how friendly both governments might be toward the United States, that either country would take any step which might embroil them with the Axis unless the other took the same line, or if Argentina, Brazil and Chile all remained neutral.

The basic issue, therefore, was whether Argentina, Brazil and Chile would decide to break relations with the Axis and prevent their territories from becoming a base for hostile acts against the United States and the other American republics that were at war.

The President of Chile had died a short time before. Under the Constitution, national elections for his successor had to be held within a period of six months. Until then the Chilean Government in power was only provisional, and for that reason, was decidedly unwilling to take any step that might end in war.

It was, therefore, highly improbable that Dr. Rossetti, the Chilean Foreign Minister, would be authorized by his Government to agree to any resolution at Rio that would alter Chile's strict neutrality before the presidential elections.

The Argentine people had already suffered the first of the many blows Fate was to deal them during that decade. Their President, Dr. Roberto Ortiz, a fervent supporter of the democracies, had been forced to resign by fatal illness. He had been succeeded by the Vice President, Dr. Castillo, a narrow reactionary and a confirmed isolationist. His Foreign Minister, Dr. Ruíz Guiñazú, who was to be Argentina's delegate at the Rio Conference, was one of the stupidest men to hold office in that great nation's history. He had admitted to me in Washington only a few months before that General Franco was his idol. He had taken no trouble to conceal the extent of his admiration for Mussolini's brand of fascism. Both he and President Castillo were subject to the influence of individuals and of interests in Argentina that were notoriously serving as Axis tools. Dr. Ruiz Guiñazú, I knew, had tried and failed to persuade Paraguay, Uruguay and Bolivia to join Argentina and Chile in a last-ditch resistance to any action by the Conference to forge a hemispheric coalition against the Axis. The foreign policy of Dr. Castillo and of Dr. Ruíz Guiñazú—if policy it could be called—had the strong support of the Argentine Army. The measures already taken to muzzle the Argentine Congress and press were making it increasingly difficult for Argentine public opinion to make itself heard.

This increasingly potent influence of the Argentine Army in deciding Argentine national policy provided the gravest complication insofar as Brazil was concerned. The rivalry between Argentina and Brazil is traditional, and at times has been acute. Because Brazil is the only South American republic that is not of Spanish origin, she has always feared that she might at some given moment find herself isolated in the midst of her Spanish-American neighbors. For that reason Brazilian foreign policy has consistently been founded, first, upon an exceptionally intimate understanding with the United States and, second, upon a close relationship with Chile, as a counterpoise to Argentina.

So long as General Justo had been President of Argentina he had co-operated wholeheartedly with President Vargas of Brazil in seeking to eliminate all causes of friction between the two neighboring countries. The same policy had been scrupulously continued by his successor, President Ortiz. But with the advent of President Castillo the situation had suddenly changed. Not only was the Argentine Army becoming all-powerful, but the president and his principal advisers were inclining more and more to extreme nationalism. There were already persistent rumors that, to deter growing opposition at home, the Argentine Army was urging the Government to embrace the doctrine of "Greater Argentina"—that is, expansion either through the relegation of Argentina's smaller neighbors to the role of protectorates, or through the seizure of additional territory.

There can be no doubt that Axis agents had sedulously spread these reports in order to frighten the Brazilian Government and persuade it not to support the United Nations, though unquestionably only a few of the more extravagant of President Castillo's advisers really believed that an expansionist policy was any longer feasible. Nevertheless, many of Brazil's military authorities were suspicious of Argentina's ulterior purposes. They were convinced that as long as Argentina remained neutral, southern Brazil would be in real danger should their Government take any step that might lead to war with the Axis. The very great influence that General von Faulhaber and other high-ranking German generals had secured over the Argentine Army during their term as military instructors was very much in their minds.

President Vargas and his brilliantly qualified Minister for Foreign Affairs, Dr. Oswaldo Aranha, together with most of the members of the Cabinet, were anxious to show their support for the United States. Their sentiments were shared by an overwhelming majority of the Brazilian people. Yet President Vargas and his Cabinet could not adopt a policy of open support for the United Nations if this were vetoed by the Brazilian Army and Navy. Nor could they forget that more than a million Germans and Italians had settled in São Paulo, in Rio Grande and in other parts of Southern Brazil, and that at least 300,000 Japanese were concentrated in one or two Brazilian states.

The decision Brazil would make was therefore the crux of the problem. The Brazilian Government would not willingly follow any line that involved a break with Argentina. But if some way could be found by which such a break could be avoided and by which Brazil might yet lead in a move for continental solidarity against the Axis, she would be warmly backed by her northern neighbors, Colombia and Venezuela, and by her southern neighbor, Uruguay. In this case Paraguay, Peru, Bolivia and Ecuador would far rather support Brazil, and stand with the United States, than adopt the policy of isolation favored by Argentina.

The coming meeting of the American foreign ministers would also demonstrate practically the capacity of the hemispheric system to take rapid action in the face of danger. Such a meeting would never have been possible had it not been for President Roosevelt's foresight in initiating a special conference for the preservation of peace in Buenos Aires in 1936. That Conference is one of the few examples of prevision to be found in the annals of American diplomacy. President Roosevelt had had two objectives in mind. The first was to set up the machinery needed to end such continental conflicts as the Chaco war, and to solve peacefully all the other quarrels that made real inter-American co-operation impossible. He wanted to create an atmosphere of hemispheric confidence in which the United States could help to perfect the New World system on which his heart was set.

The second objective was still more far-reaching. By the early winter of 1936 the President had become convinced that France and Great Britain would be unwilling or unable to prevent the rapid rise of a militaristic Germany under the Nazis. He believed a Second World War was looming. The New World must be put in order so that when the crisis came the Americas at least might stand united.

There was no little grim humor in remembering that after the President and I had discussed the most effective way to attain these objectives, Secretary Hull had opposed any conference in 1936 on the ground we might as well wait for the regular Pan-American Conference in 1938, and that anyhow the Latin Americans were bound to ask us for the moon!

Yet the conference of 1936 had achieved precisely what the President wanted. By going in person to make the opening address he had deeply impressed the entire continent. He had won for the United States a measure of real friendship among the Latin-American peoples that would have seemed incredible during the Hoover Administration. He had impressed upon all the Latin-American leaders with whom he talked the dangers he saw in the European situation and the imperative necessity for the American nations to pull together. He urged the need for the rest of the world to be shown what an international relationship based upon justice and peace could do for humanity.

By unanimously adopting a resolution introduced at that conference by the five Central American countries, the American republics had endorsed the principle that any threat to the peace of one American nation would be considered a threat to every other American nation. This agreement, further developed at subsequent Pan-American conferences, was responsible for the meeting of foreign ministers now to take place at Rio de Janeiro. Without the Conference of 1936, there would have been little chance for hemispheric co-operation after Pearl Harbor.

It was at the 1936 Conference that Secretary Hull first developed that violent antipathy to Argentina which was later to become an obsession. Argentina's Foreign Minister at that time had been Dr. Carlos Saavedra Lamas. He was a brilliant and enlightened statesman, but his fear of United States preponderance made him stubbornly oppose any political organization of the Americas. He was further convinced that Argentina's interest lay in her ties with Europe, notably with Great Britain, and in developing her role as a world power rather than as merely one member of an American system.

I remembered vividly the climactic meeting between Mr. Hull and Dr. Saavedra Lamas at the Anchorena Palace in Buenos Aires, at which Ambassador Espil and I served as interpreters (neither of the foreign ministers could speak the other's language), and my persistent effort in my translation to temper

Mr. Hull's aspersions upon the views and conduct of Dr. Saavedra Lamas, in order to prevent an open brawl.

Another lasting grievance of Mr. Hull's was that although he had supported Dr. Saavedra Lamas' candidacy for the Nobel Peace Prize, the Argentine Foreign Minister failed to see him off when he sailed at the end of the Conference.

His prejudice against Argentina was later exacerbated by her unwillingness blindly to follow his lead at the Pan-American Conference at Lima in 1938. When I served as United States delegate at the Inter-American Conference in Panama in 1939, he refused to credit my assertion that I received the full and very friendly co-operation of the Argentine Delegation.

Argentina's bitter opposition to the development of a political system of the Americas has frequently proved frustrating. It undeniably retarded the development of the hemispheric machinery needed to make the regional system work. But the very foundation of the inter-American system was the United States' acceptance of the juridical equality of all the American republics. From that standpoint, particularly since no inter-American conference could yet take action except by unanimous agreement, it was illogical to regard Argentina as hostile to the United States merely because her policy differed diametrically from our own. Unfortunately, however, the anti-Argentine bias with which Mr. Hull was by now seized had already become almost psychopathic.

In my last talk with the President the afternoon before I left Washington for Rio de Janeiro, we discussed Mr. Hull's antipathy to Argentina at some length. I suspect that the President occasionally, in the spirit of sheer mischief he sometimes showed, goaded Mr. Hull when the question of Argentina came up.

I went over with the President the chief points in my opening address, which the Secretary of State had already approved. I emphasized particularly the view of the Army and Navy, as given to me by General Marshall and Admiral Stark, that the United States should discourage any further declarations of war against the Axis. They insisted that, if belligerent territory in the New World were extended, the United States had neither sufficient force nor matériel to cope with possible Axis retaliation. My primary objective therefore was to get all the American republics to agree on a joint breach of relations with the Axis, and further, to agree upon measures necessary to prevent any part of the continent from becoming a base for subversive activities against the American countries that were already at war.

The President approved of the course that I had marked out. He asked me what I thought Argentina would do. I replied that the constitutional difficulties in Chile would make it easier for Argentina to insist that no definite step be taken at this time. But I also said that, if Brazil and her other neighbors wished to support the United States, I doubted whether, even under her present Government, Argentina would be willing to find herself isolated.

I said that it seemed to me the expedient course was for us to lay the facts before our American neighbors, and to avoid taking any action that would break the unity of the hemisphere and thereby give the Axis a chance to fish in muddy waters. The President gave me his wholehearted approval. As I left, he wished me "good luck" with that smile and characteristic wave of the hand which one so gratefully remembers as one now looks back over the years when the White House was illuminated by his great heart and great spirit.

In summing up my balance sheet I felt I had one other invaluable advantage. That was the nature of the United States press delegation that went with me to the Rio de Janeiro Conference. Needless to say, I would have been as unwilling to offer the press and radio correspondents any suggestion about the kind of reports they should send as they would have been unwilling to receive them. As a matter of record, throughout the Conference I reported to them fully every development, whether confidential or not. It is my belief that the United States press can, if it is given the chance, do as much to further the aims of our foreign policy as our official diplomacy. By reporting the facts accurately and objectively, the press can make it possible for the American public to know not only what that policy is, but—what is quite as important—the reasons for it.

On this plane trip, in talking with the American correspondents accompanying our delegation, I had told them that, in view of the dangerous situation in which the whole Western Hemisphere now found itself, the Argentine Government could not be permitted to jeopardize our common safety by preventing other American republics from co-operating to protect the Americas. But I tried at the same time to make it equally clear that, granted the achievement of this major objective, the preservation of hemispheric unity must remain paramount.

I suddenly realized that the regular rise and fall of the plane had changed to a series of rapid and shuddering jolts. A solid mass of water streamed over the windows as we passed through a torrential rain cloud. Far down below I caught a glimpse of Rio's familiar and incomparable harbor. With one huge gray wing dipping, we circled around and around. At length we came slowly down.

Then came the official welcome in the midst of an unruly and enthusiastic crowd. Then the dash, with blaring sirens, through Rio's crowded boulevards at seventy miles an hour to the Copacabana Hotel.

In retrospect those first days seem as kaleidoscopic as the race from the airport to the hotel.

On the way down the foreign ministers of Mexico, Colombia and Venezuela had shown me a draft resolution providing for an immediate break by the American republics of all relations with the Axis. This resolution soon received the support of a large number of other delegates, including Dr. Guani, the representative of Uruguay, who courageously made his own country's attitude clear at the first session of the Conference.

The Brazilian Foreign Minister, Dr. Oswaldo Aranha, rapidly assumed leadership in an effort to secure adherence of all the remaining delegations to this resolution. The President of Peru, Dr. Manuel Prado, telephoned me through his brother, who was then Peruvian Ambassador in Rio de Janeiro, that the Government of Peru had decided to support it. In a series of conferences which I had with the foreign ministers of Bolivia, Ecuador and Paraguay I was given the promise that, in view of the position taken by Brazil, their governments would also support it.

Of course, I also talked often with the foreign ministers of Argentina and of Chile. I had reason to believe from my conversations with the latter that Chile was by no means intransigent, provided the text of the resolution could be modified to provide that the severance of relations with the Axis powers must be undertaken in accordance with each republic's constitutional procedure. To this amendment there could, of course, be no objection, particularly in the case of Chile, who had as yet no elected President.

I had, however, received no such encouragement from the Argentine Foreign Minister. He refused to make any commitment to me, and in our talks frequently brought up his favorite argument that the Japanese attack had taken place against Hawaii, a group of islands in the middle of the Pacific, and the mere fact that the United States flag flew over the territory did not mean that Japan had attacked the Americas; consequently none of the American republics had any moral obligation to join in preserving the peace of the New World. It therefore came as a welcome surprise when Dr. Aranha informed me with much satisfaction on January 23 that Dr. Ruíz Guiñazú had agreed to sign a resolution which called upon each American republic to break relations with the Axis.

Many of the delegates immediately met in Dr. Aranha's room in the Brazilian Foreign Office to draft the final text. The Argentine Foreign Minister and several members of his delegation haggled for a while over this or that word, but after a long time had been spent in this debate, they withdrew their insistence upon amendments which would have defeated the fundamental purpose of the resolution and agreed to a text that was equivalent to the one originally presented.

At my daily meeting with the American correspondents that same evening I told them that the radical differences that had existed at the opening of the Conference seemed now to have vanished. I said I thought that on the following day the resolution for a break of relations with the Axis would be introduced into the Conference by all twenty-one delegates, including the delegate of Argentina.

Early the next morning Dr. Aranha telephoned me to come to see him as soon as possible. Upon my arrival at his office he told me that the Argentine Foreign Minister's commitment had been overruled by his President, and that the Conference was facing a chaotic condition.

I asked at once what stand the Brazilian Government would take. He replied that the influences opposing any step that might lead Brazil into war if Argentina remained aloof were so strong that he did not think President Vargas could now follow the course he had planned. The only possible solution lay in working out a resolution that would retain what was essential and that the Argentine Government would accept.

President Roosevelt had liked and had had great confidence in President Vargas since his visit to Rio de Janeiro in 1936. I myself had entire faith in his desire to give the United States all possible support. I asked Dr. Aranha if he would arrange a confidential interview for me with his President.

A few hours later President Vargas received me in his secret hide-out on the top of the mountain peak that rises back of the gardens of the Cattete Palace. Our talk could hardly have been franker. Dr. Vargas has a singularly impassive face but he talks freely to those he trusts. He referred to his increasing difficulties with Argentina since the days of President Justo and of President Ortiz, and to the belief of most of his head Army and Navy officers that the safety of Brazil's southern frontiers could not be guaranteed if she suddenly found herself at war with the Axis while Argentina was neutral. He made it clear that, were Brazil to take action against the Axis, she must in any event receive from the United States the mechanized equipment and munitions of which the Brazilian Army was desperately short.

I told him that I had already cabled President Roosevelt about these requirements. I could give the Brazilian Government a list of the matériel that President Roosevelt had told me would at once be made available to Brazil notwithstanding the demands of our own services and of our allies.

President Vargas then, without emotion, but with extreme gravity, explained how great he felt his personal responsibility to be. He emphasized the magnitude of the dangers to which Brazil would be exposed unless the United States committed herself, in spirit as well as in act, to help defend Brazil if the need arose. These dangers would in any case be insuperable unless the Conference could find some formula that the Argentine Government would support. He gave me his positive assurance that if this effort proved successful, Brazil would announce before the conclusion of the Conference that she had broken her relations with the Axis countries.

After I had cabled Washington of these new developments I returned to the Brazilian Foreign Office. There I met with most of the other chief delegates. Indignant as they were at the new turn of events, and at the reasons for it, they were as one in believing that the solidarity of the hemisphere must be preserved. They felt that the Axis would secure an immense advantage from the breakup of the inter-American system that would occur should the Conference end with an open breach between Argentina and Chile on the one side and the remaining nineteen republics on the other. The short-range dangers to the rest of the continent from the untrammeled activities of

Axis agents in the two southernmost republics would be extreme. The long-range danger was the probability that all chances for the growth of a workable regional organization would be destroyed.

When the Argentine delegates arrived, formula after formula was brought up only to be rejected. After many fruitless hours the Argentine Foreign Minister and his Chilean colleague said they could obtain the consent of their Governments to a formula that "recommended" that each American republic sever all relations with the Axis. Such a resolution was obviously neither so clear-cut nor so peremptory as the earlier version. Yet in reality there was no essential difference.

The Argentine Constitution in force in 1942 was still very like that of the United States. Under it the Argentine Executive alone has the power to break relations with other states. If the Argentine Foreign Minister, with the approval of the executive branch of his Government, now "recommended" that Argentina break relations with the Axis, any failure by the Argentine Executive to carry out that recommendation would be a violation of an official commitment to all the other American republics.

Dr. Aranha, Dr. Padilla, the Mexican Minister of Foreign Affairs, Dr. Parra Pérez, the Venezuelan Foreign Minister, as well as several other delegates who had been responsible for the original resolution, all approved this substitute formula; it would preserve the unity of the hemisphere and still result in that joint breach of relations with the Axis which they felt to be imperative.

The responsibility now rested with me. I did not see that there would be any advantage to the United States in opposing this new resolution merely because its language was not so decisive as that earlier suggested, President Vargas had left no doubt in my mind that even though he wanted to give full support to the United States, Brazil would not break relations unless the Argentine Republic was equally committed. Nor was there any doubt that if Brazil postponed taking this step, Peru, Bolivia, Ecuador and Paraguay would also delay action. If all the southern republics refused to move, the threat of successful *coups d'etat* in South America would be much greater. The activities of the Axis and Fascist *saboteurs* in many of these countries would continue to be uncontrolled. The menace to South Atlantic and Caribbean shipping would grow, and our own safety would be increasingly jeopardized.

From the larger viewpoint—the permanent interests of the New World—would the United States be warranted in destroying the unity of the twenty-one American nations, when she knew that under the conditions then existing the break must be bitter and long? Would it be the part of true statesmanship, solely in order that the hemisphere's most powerful Government, the United States, might gain its immediate objective, to "crack down" on another sovereign country whose people had little responsibility for their government's policies? Could such an act fail to arouse popular resentment that would linger long after the reasons for the "cracking down" had been forgotten? Would the enlightened leaders of public opinion in other Latin-American countries have felt we were justified in taking a step that inevitably implied the postponement or even the abandonment of the inter-American system that they had all come to regard as of vital value? To me the answer to all of these questions was then, as it remains today, an unhesitating "no."

Realizing that any delay in my decision would give the power-

ful pro-Axis forces in Buenos Aires a new chance to persuade
the Argentine Government again to change its mind, I said that
the United States would join in the unanimous endorsement
of the formula now agreed upon.

This final formula read as follows:

The American Republics reaffirm their complete solidarity and
their determination to cooperate jointly for their mutual protection
until the effects of the present aggression against the continent have
disappeared.

The American Republics, in accordance with the procedures established by their own laws and in conformity with the position and
circumstances obtaining in each country in the existing continental
conflict, recommend the breaking of their diplomatic relations with
Japan, Germany and Italy, since the first-mentioned state attacked,
and the other two declared war on, an American country.

Within a few moments all of the twenty-one delegates had
signed this text. It was immediately presented to the Political
Committee of the Conference, in accordance with the Conference rules, so that it might then be formally adopted at a
plenary session.

At a meeting with our own press correspondents soon after,
I explained as fully as I could, without disclosing the confidential
talk I had had with President Vargas, the difficulties that had
arisen and the compromise solution that had at length been
reached. I emphasized my belief that this compromise had not
only preserved the unity of the hemisphere but that it also assured
the achievement of our major objectives. Most of the United
States correspondents, who had a thoroughly realistic grasp of the
essentials in inter-American relations, and who appraised accurately the dangers of a break between Argentina and Chile and

the rest of the continent, sent their newspapers objective reports of what had happened. I later learned, however, that a few, notably Mr. Allen Hayden, then a correspondent for the Chicago *Daily News,* who were vehement exponents of a "crack down" on Argentina policy, cabled up stories asserting that the Argentine Government had succeeded in preventing the Conference from agreeing on a break in relations with the Axis. It was alleged that the United States had received the most ignominious diplomatic defeat in its history.

I had to spend all that evening at the Brazilian Foreign Office, since I was a member of the Mediation Commission that was trying to find a definitive solution of the Peruvian-Ecuadorean boundary dispute before the conference adjourned. At last, after almost forty-eight hours of uninterrupted work, I was able to get back at midnight to my rooms for what I hoped would be a night's sleep.

I had hardly got into bed before the telephone rang. Secretary Hull was calling from Washington. I subsequently was told by the late Laurence Duggan that after reading one or two of the press reports claiming a "diplomatic triumph" for Argentina, Mr. Hull had summoned a few of his closest advisers to his apartment. It was from there that he called me. Without any preliminary amenities and his voice quivering with fury, the Secretary of State said, "You have got us into a fine mess. I never gave you *carte blanche* to act for us."

He then continued by telling me that at the first possible moment on the following morning I was to inform the Conference that I had not been authorized by my Government to agree to the compromise resolution that I had approved, and to announce that the United States would oppose it. As soon as I was able to get

a word in I tried to the best of my ability to remind the Secretary
that I had received specific authority from President Roosevelt
to take precisely the action I had taken. I pointed out that if the
United States were now to withdraw the approval already given,
the Conference would inevitably collapse, with nothing but benefit to the Axis. Inter-American unity would be shattered, with
grave danger to ourselves. Because of internal conditions, Brazil
would be unable to make any immediate break, and in that case
neither Ecuador, Peru, Bolivia nor Paraguay, would be willing to
move. I reminded him that the Brazilian Government had assured
me that, in view of our approval of a resolution which avoided a
clash between Argentina and Brazil, it would announce that
Brazil had broken relations with the Axis before the end of the
Conference, and that I had received similar pledges from the
governments of Uruguay, Paraguay, Bolivia, Ecuador and Peru.
To this latter statement Mr. Hull's sole rejoinder was that I was
indeed ingenuous if I had been "taken in" by any such promises
as these, and that I would find that not one of these governments
would carry out their commitments.

When I found that no arguments and no requests for recon-
sideration were of the slightest avail, I told Mr. Hull that I felt
it was necessary for me to appeal personally to the President. In
my judgment the issue at stake involved the vital safety of the
United States at a time of acute peril, and the consequences of
the instructions he had given me could only be disastrous. The
authority I exercised I had received directly from the President.
I could not reverse my position unless the President personally
instructed me to do so.

Luckily the President was in the White House. A three-way
conversation then took place. It was evident from the start (and

the President confirmed this upon my return) that the Secretary of State had already been bombarding him with demands that my action be disavowed. At the outset Secretary Hull went over the situation, insisting that Argentina must be treated as an "outlaw." To this statement the President made no reply. He asked me to explain my own point of view, and to give him the picture as I saw it, and the reasons why I felt it essential that the compromise resolution be accepted. I went over the situation as briefly as I could. I emphasized that the position of the Brazilian Government was the key to the whole problem, that unless Brazil could prevent divergent policies in Buenos Aires and Rio de Janeiro, it would be difficult, if not impossible, for her to break relations, and that in this case most of her neighbors would feel compelled to follow her example. I said I was convinced that the safety of the hemisphere during our own struggle with the Axis was at stake and I itemized the dangers that were bound to arise if inter-American unity were destroyed.

President Roosevelt, without hesitation, then made the following statement: "I am sorry, Cordell, but in this case I am going to take the judgment of the man on the spot." Talking to me, he said, "Sumner, I approve what you have done. I authorize you to follow the lines you have recommended."

Mr. Hull was silent. The conversation ended.

In Mr. Hull's book of reminiscences he presents a misleading report of this conversation. He says that the President's approval of my course was due to his belief that "it would not be feasible to reconsider the action Welles had taken." The President's exact words were, as I have above recorded, "In this case I am going to take the judgment of the man on the spot."

Mr. Hull fails to mention the internal difficulties faced by the

Government of Brazil. He omits any reference to my statement to him and to the President that, if Brazil found it impossible at that moment to break relations, most of her smaller neighbors would probably also postpone action. He further refrains from reporting his own assertion to me that Brazil and her neighbors would fail to carry out their promise to sever relations with the Axis if the compromise resolution were adopted by the Conference.

In his book Mr. Hull speaks of the Conference as "this failure at Rio."

History has long since shown up the glaring inaccuracy of that appraisal. Before the end of the Conference nineteen American republics were at war or had broken their relations with the Axis and long before V-E Day the two remaining republics had followed suit. The security of the United States and of the hemisphere had been safeguarded. Antagonism between Argentina and Chile and their neighbors had been prevented. The unity of the hemisphere had been preserved. The preservation of that unity has today made it possible for the Organization of the American States to exist. That regional system has been and will continue to be one of the strongest pillars upon which the structure of the United Nations rests.

The fact that a series of military dictatorships seized power in Argentina after the Rio Conference of 1942, and the policies of the Government subsequently elected have overclouded the real issues involved in this question. Recent events in Argentina have caused many to forget that the acts of governments are transitory while relations between peoples are lasting. In the long run the people of the United States will gain infinitely more from an inter-American system based on tolerance, understanding and friendship than they would have gained from a decision by their Government in 1942 to put Argentina and Chile "in their place," and ostracize two great countries from the American family of nations.

In the admirably fair and objective review of Mr. Hull's book written by Professor Arthur P. Whitaker of the University of Pennsylvania, he states in the conclusion, "It may be suggested . . . that any Secretary of State who insists upon making his own decisions upon Latin American policy should first be required to have a thorough grounding in Latin American history."

In another part of the same review the statement is made: "Toward the close of Hull's term his Pan American policies were among his least successful policies."

The truth is that Mr. Hull was devoid not only of any knowledge of Latin-American history, but also of the language and culture of our American neighbors. He had no understanding of Latin-American psychology. He had little grasp of the social and economic problems that the Latin-American republics presently confront.

He accomplished a great service for hemispheric understanding by the position that he at first took in behalf of nonintervention. He did it an equally great disservice when in his last years as Secretary of State he continually insisted on a policy of direct interference in the internal concerns of the Argentine people.

On the day following my fateful talk with Washington, the Conference gave formal approval to the compromise resolution. On the same day the governments of Peru and Uruguay announced that they had broken relations with the Axis. On the two succeeding days the governments of Bolivia and of Paraguay made similar announcements. In his closing address as Chairman of the Conference, Dr. Aranha announced to the Conference and to the world that Brazil had one hour before severed her relations with Germany, Italy and Japan. The Government of Ecuador then made known that it had taken the same step. The elected Government of Chile that came to power a few months later broke relations with the Axis within the year. After a number of political upheavals, in the course of which her constitutional Government was overthrown and a series of military dictatorships succeeded each other in power, Argentina finally followed suit at the beginning of the year following.

I flew back to Washington the morning after the conference adjourned. Upon my return to the State Department, Secretary Hull refused to see me or to give me any briefing of what had taken place during the three weeks of my absence at one of the most critical periods in our history. He later left for Florida. He remained immured for nearly three months.

The significance of the decision reached by President Roosevelt in that tripartite telephone conversation in the night of January 25, 1942, can hardly be overestimated. Its consequences helped to insure the safety of the United States and augmented our ability effectively to prosecute the war in Europe as well as in the Pacific.

Had the Government of Brazil been unwilling to break relation with the Axis when it did, the many powerful elements that believed a policy of strict neutrality was expedient would have become increasingly powerful. As time went on it would have been more and more difficult for the Brazilian Government to take the decisive step. The Nazi Government would undoubtedly have used every possible precaution to avoid all provocation.

Under a policy of rigid neutrality Brazil could not have offered us the use of her ports for our South Atlantic fleet. Without them we could never have patrolled the South Atlantic effectively, where as it was German U-boats sank in 1942 more American and British shipping bound for Russia and Britain's North African armies than in any other area.

What is still more important, the Brazilian Government could not have permitted the United States to build in northern Brazil the airfields that were essential to the development of our air transport flights across Central Africa to Egypt and the Mediterranean. Without these airfields the invasion of Algeria and of Morocco could not have taken place in November, 1942.

American public opinion would naturally have been aroused against the South American republics that refused to support the United States by breaking relations with the Axis. The acrimonious attacks and counterattacks in the press, on the radio, in public forums, and in official quarters would have so poisoned the atmosphere that pro-Axis sentiment in South America would have grown rapidly, even in countries where public opinion had previously been strongly pro-Ally. Under those conditions, no matter how effective our Intelligence Service in Latin America might have been, it would have been impossible to prevent the sabotage of allied shipping, and a probable series of *coups d'etat* that would have installed pro-Axis governments in several American republics. Finally, if those conditions had continued until V-J Day, we would have found ourselves part of a hemisphere that was torn with internecine rivalries, increasingly antagonistic to us and unprepared to present a solid front in the present contest with the Soviet Union.

In the long list of outstanding contributions that President Roosevelt made to the cause of inter-American understanding and friendship, and to the construction of an enduring regional system, surely none has proved of more permanent value than that made during the Conference of the Ministers of Foreign Relations in Rio de Janeiro in January, 1942.

CHAPTER V

The Decision to Postpone Political and Territorial Decisions until after the War

WALTER LIPPMANN came to see me late one afternoon in what was then my office as Under Secretary of
State in the old State, War and Navy Building. It was a warm
day in the early spring of 1942. There was a misty haze of green
over the elms of the Ellipse. Through the open windows you
could see the Potomac shining beyond the barracks that had been
hastily put up after Pearl Harbor for the White House guard.
From his portrait above my desk Andrew Jackson's somber and
brooding eyes gazed across the room at the likeness of his great
antagonist, John Quincy Adams. After hours the office seemed
an oasis in the turmoil that then was Washington.

Lippmann had come in to get some news about the latest development in our Vichy policy, to which he was vigorously
opposed. Before leaving he said that if I had a few minutes free
he wanted to talk about another matter that seemed to him of
supreme importance.

He reminded me that while during the First World War
President Wilson's Fourteen Points had dealt in general terms
with some political and territorial problems, the Allies had
reached no accord on detailed settlements before the Armistice.
He believed this was one of the chief reasons why so many of the

decisions made at the Paris Peace Conference were unsound and unwise. They were often entered into hastily and without proper study or knowledge. If they involved the interests of one of the major allies, they usually represented a weak compromise between what the negotiators knew was right and what the power most directly affected wanted.

This time, Lippmann added, all we had to fall back on was the Atlantic Charter, recently embodied in the United Nations Declaration. The Charter was far less specific even than the Wilson Fourteen Points. He knew, of course, that we were already trying within the State Department to work out our own conclusions about the new peace settlements. What he wanted to find out was whether we intended to try to reach agreements on these questions with other members of the United Nations while the war was still in progress.

He took it for granted that the provinces seized from France by Germany and Italy would be restored to her, and that Czechoslovakia would regain her territorial integrity. But what about such complex and difficult questions as the postwar frontiers of Rumania and of Hungary; what about the still more intricate problem of Poland, now that the Soviet Union, which had seized half of Poland's prewar territory, was one of our own allies; what about the future status of the Baltic states, whose independence the Soviet Union had obliterated; and, above all else, what about the future frontiers of Germany and the kind of Germany there was going to be?

I could only answer that I believed the President and his Secretary of State were officially committed to a policy of no agreements on territorial adjustments or political settlements until

after the war, when they could be dealt with at a peace conference of the United Nations. I said I believed this was also very
definitely the policy favored by the Foreign Relations Committee of the Senate.

I will always remember that afternoon. I was naturally not able
to say that I was strongly opposed to the position taken on this
question by the Administration in which I served and wholeheartedly in agreement with the views of my visitor. I was profoundly impressed with the gravity of the problem. And there
was little I could do. The decision was based almost entirely on
military factors in whose evaluation I played no part.

I was at that very moment studying afresh the records of the
Paris Peace Conference of 1919, and I was engrossed in departmental discussions of precisely such territorial and political questions as those Walter Lippmann had raised. The more I read
about the negotiations of 1919, the more I was convinced that our
wisest course would be to try to work out with our allies now,
before V-Day, as detailed an agreement as possible. Our armed
strength, our material resources, the moral authority of President
Roosevelt and, even more perhaps, our allies' need of us, would
give us infinitely greater leverage now than we could have after
the victory was won.

Experience had shown during the Paris Conference of 1919—
even though we were then dealing primarily with Great Britain,
France and Italy, all Western nations—how appallingly difficult
it was to overcome the exaggerated forms of selfish nationalism
to which a victorious war gives rise. This time we would be dealing with the Soviet Union. The Kremlin's course following the
Stalin-Hitler deal in August, 1939, hardly gave ground for con-

fidence in the inherent altruism of the Politburo's foreign policy. There was little reason to think that after the defeat of Germany and Italy a triumphant Russia would be disposed to give the just claims of humanity priority over her own demands for what Stalin would term "security." If the great peace conferences of Vienna in 1815 and of Paris in 1919 had taught any one lesson clearly, it was surely this: that victorious allies invariably quarrel among themselves over the division of the spoils.

In this case, all the "spoils" that the United States wanted for herself was a peace founded on justice and practical common sense so that future wars might be avoided. But we would hardly be likely to attain this single end if we postponed action until the quarrels of the victors had again broken out around the peace table.

Yet the possibility of such action seemed to be precluded at the outset. Early in December, 1941, Anthony Eden, then Britain's Foreign Secretary, was about to go to Moscow. Though the United States was not yet at war, he had let us know that the future status of the Baltic republics would undoubtedly come up in his talks with Stalin and Molotov. I myself expressed the strong hope in talking with the President and Secretary Hull that we would urge the British Government not to make any final agreement that would commit Great Britain to support the permanent obliteration of Lithuania, Latvia and Estonia. A message in that sense was sent to Mr. Eden through Ambassador Winant in London.

But the message sent by Secretary Hull went much farther indeed than a mere note of caution on this specific issue. The position he took was that, since the Soviet, British and United

States governments had bound themselves to be guided by the Atlantic Charter in all postwar settlements, no specific terms of settlement should be agreed upon before the final peace conference. The Secretary of State very properly concluded by also urging that in any event no secret commitments should be made.

At the moment when the message was sent (only two days before Pearl Harbor) the terms in which it was couched seemed innocuous enough. The principles for postwar policy laid down by the Atlantic Charter provided an altogether desirable pattern. Yet they constituted a pattern, and nothing more. They gave no slightest indication, for example, of the justice or injustice of a given settlement covering eastern Poland. The Soviet Union might claim quite plausibly that her retention of eastern Poland would not be territorial aggrandizement of the sort prohibited by the first article of the Atlantic Charter, but, on the contrary, a "territorial change" that fully accorded "with the freely expressed wishes of the peoples concerned," as authorized by the second article. Yet the Polish Government-in-Exile would inevitably maintain that such a "territorial change" was aggrandizement at its worst, and that the wishes of "the peoples concerned" could not be "freely expressed." Agreement upon the broad principles of the Atlantic Charter would never in itself prevent future bitter controversies over frontiers and zones of influence.

In any event, the message of December 5, 1941, to Anthony Eden created a precedent upon which a policy was soon erected. When Mr. Eden left for Moscow he took with him instructions from his Cabinet that were similar in intent to the request made by the United States Government. In Moscow, however, he was met with an insistent demand that Great Britain without further ado formally commit herself to the recognition of Russia's 1941 frontiers as established by Stalin's 1939 deal with Hitler.

According to Mr. Eden,[1] Stalin also

. . . proposed the restoration of Austria as an independent state, the detachment of the Rhineland from Prussia as an independent state or protectorate, and possibly the constitution of an independent state of Bavaria. He also proposed that East Prussia should be transferred to Poland and the Sudetenland returned to Czechoslovakia. He suggested that Yugoslavia should be restored, and even receive certain additional territories from Italy; that Albania should be reconstituted as an independent state and that Turkey should receive the Dodecanese, with possible adjustments in favor of Greece as regards islands in the Aegean important to Greece. Turkey might also receive certain districts in Bulgaria and possibly also in northern Syria. In general, the occupied countries, including Czechoslovakia and Greece, should be restored to their pre-war frontiers. . . . As regards the special interests of the Soviet Union, Stalin desired the restoration of the position in 1941, prior to the German attack, in respect of the Baltic States, Finland and Bessarabia. The "Curzon Line" should form the basis for the future Soviet-Polish frontier, and Rumania should give special facilities for bases, etc., to the Soviet Union, receiving compensation from territory now occupied by Hungary.

Stalin later insisted that British recognition of the Soviet's demands concerning her 1941 frontiers must be a preliminary to any Anglo-Soviet treaty of alliance.

In accordance with his instructions, Mr. Eden limited himself to the promise that the Russian claims would at some future time be considered by the British Commonwealth as well as by the United States. But upon his return to London he was further pressed by Mr. Molotov for a categorical acceptance of the Rus-

[1] Churchill, Winston, *The Grand Alliance* (Boston: Houghton Mifflin Co., 1950), p. 629.

sian demands. It appeared from Mr. Eden's messages that he was impressed with the need to comply, unless the English-speaking powers were willing to risk an early break with their Soviet ally and a separate peace treaty between the Soviet Union and the Nazi Government.

The issue was, of course, clear-cut. It was evident that even at the climax of the furious German assault upon the Soviet armies Stalin wished to be sure that he would retain the fruits of his earlier collusion with Hitler. The Soviet Government had just subscribed to the United Nations Declaration and, consequently, to the provisions of the Atlantic Charter. Yet it was now pressing for a commitment that, certainly in the case of the Baltic states, would violate the spirit as well as the letter of the Charter.

From our standpoint in Washington such an agreement was unthinkable. Our acquiescence in it would have been interpreted in every quarter of the globe as meaning that the Atlantic Charter was, in fact, no more than a hollow sham, a collection of high-sounding phrases designed merely to impress the ingenuous. It would have lost the United States that invaluable measure of moral support which she was given in every country where people were still able to think and speak freely, and which eventually proved to be of such great avail in winning the war.

We found that Mr. Churchill stood four-square with us on this issue. He stated flatly then, during his first visit to Washington as Prime Minister, what he has since frequently reiterated, "The Baltic States should be sovereign independent peoples." In a message to Mr. Eden of January 8, 1942, he said[2]:

The transfer of the peoples of the Baltic States to Soviet Russia against their will would be contrary to all the principles for which

[2] *Ibid.*, p. 695.

we are fighting this war and would dishonor our cause. This also applies to Bessarabia and to Northern Bukhovina and in a lesser degree to Finland, which I gather it is not intended wholly to subjugate and absorb. . . . In any case there can be no question of settling frontiers until the peace conference. I know President Roosevelt holds this view as strongly as I do, and he has several times expressed his pleasure to me at the firm line we took at Moscow. . . . There must be no mistake about the opinion of any British Government of which I am the head, namely, that it adheres to those principles of freedom and democracy set forth in the Atlantic Charter, and that these principles must become especially active whenever any question of transferring territory is raised.

Thus, barely a month after the United States entered the war, the American and British governments reached a firm agreement that no commitments upon postwar political and territorial settlements should be made until the peace conference. For the time being the Soviet Government acquiesced. When Molotov visited Washington six months later in June, 1942, he made no demand that the American and British reconsider their refusal to recognize Russia's frontiers prior to June, 1941.

Yet it was, of course, inconceivable that some of our smaller allies who had territorial or political problems should not try during the war to get by direct negotiation a settlement that would be confirmed after the victory. If any demonstration of this had been needed, it was soon afforded, first, by the several visits to Washington of General Sikorski, the Prime Minister of the Polish Government-in-Exile, and, later, by the visits of President Beneš of Czechoslovakia.

Sikorski I found one of the most stalwart and attractive statesmen of the war years, and I conferred with him at great length during his weeks in Washington. He recognized, of course, as he told me repeatedly, that no final commitments on the future status of Poland or the future extension of Polish territory could be made by any Polish Government-in-Exile, but must await the freely expressed decision of the Polish people themselves. Nevertheless, he felt he would be criminally short-sighted not to try during the war to reach an agreement with the Soviet Union and with Czechoslovakia on political and territorial issues, so that the entire problem could be successfully clarified before any peace conference was held.

He foresaw, and correctly I think, no difficulty in finding an agreement with Czechoslovakia, notwithstanding the previous Polish Government's dastardly seizure of Czechoslovakian territory when Hitler occupied that country. Whether he was equally justified in speaking so confidently, on the basis of his conversations with Stalin in Moscow in 1941, of his ability to negotiate a fair settlement with the Soviet Union is another matter. I remember he told me that Stalin had, with apparent approval, quoted to him Lenin's remark that the Soviet Government must realize that the Poles had reason to hate Russia, and that consequently the Bolshevik Revolution must treat the Poles in a friendly way, and give Polish nationalism full recognition.

In any event, Sikorski succeeded, with British help, in restoring diplomatic relations between his own Government-in-Exile and Moscow, and arranged for the formation of a Polish Army to fight against Germany on Russian soil. He felt then that he had concrete evidence that he was not unduly optimistic in believing that fair political and territorial adjustments might be negotiated with Stalin.

President Beneš, because of his greater experience in the international arena, was far less sanguine. He recognized, as he told me, that the future independence and security of Czechoslovakia lay solely in her ability to walk the tightrope over the abyss between the East and the West. For that reason he made his wartime visits to Moscow, believing that only through an understanding with Stalin could his country hope to be saved from Russian hegemony in the years to come.

While I have cited only the two cases of Poland and Czechoslovakia, almost all our smaller allies spoke to me of this, that or the other territorial rectification or reparation which they hoped to consolidate by agreement before the end of the war.

As I have said, the question whether the United States was not losing an unparalleled opportunity to ensure the kind of peace that the American people wanted was much in my own mind during the two years after Pearl Harbor. By the spring of 1942 we have already commenced within the State Department our intensive study of the kind of world organization and of the kind of political and territorial settlements that we wanted to see made. But necessarily our decisions represented merely what we Americans believed to be wise, right and just. We could assume that our views coincided largely with those of the British Commonwealth, of our neighbors of the Western Hemisphere and of the lesser powers of Western Europe. But in the light of our past experience with the Soviet Union, what possible assurance could we have that at the peace conference Moscow would accept even a small percentage of our recommendations? Would it not be wise, as soon as our own views were formed and we learned what the views of our American neighbors and of some of the smaller European countries were, to try to do exactly what Mrs. Roosevelt had suggested three years before, namely, set up officially an international group "continuously to plan for future peace"?

Should we not create a body, similar in composition to what later became the Security Council of the United Nations, and representing all the United Nations, to begin without delay to study the future structure of the world, to iron out as far as possible difficulties among its member nations, and to be prepared at the end of the war to present for the final approval of the peace conference a series of settlements and of postwar policies already agreed upon in principle?

I naturally discussed this possibility with the other members of the Advisory Committee on Post-War Foreign Policy in the Department of State. There the suggestion met with general approval, enthusiastic on the part of some and tepid on the part of others. Yet at the highest level it was summarily turned down.

I think it is wholly accurate to say that, while the President decided to reject the proposal, the intrinsic idea commended itself to him. In judging his decision we must remember the influences that were being brought to bear upon him, and the considerations by which as Commander-in-Chief he must be guided. Winning the war was and must remain the foremost objective. No step could be taken politically, however beneficial it might promise to be later on, if it jeopardized or threatened to postpone the victory.

The first ten months of 1942 were for us the darkest period of the war. We had to face not only the succession of disasters that had struck us in the Pacific, but the series of calamities—such as the setbacks in Libya, the occupation of Greece, the fall of Crete, and the growing threat to the security of Egypt—that had attended the British war effort since Pearl Harbor. The Russian armies were magnificently resisting the German onslaught, but how long could they hold?

It was altogether natural that the Joint Chiefs of Staff should constantly warn the President that, whatever the theoretical future advantages of trying to settle political and territorial problems during the war, they were offset by the immediate dangers of the controversies with Russia that might be aroused. In any such attempt, we would run headlong, probably immediately, into a renewed demand that we recognize Russia's 1941 frontiers. How could we comply, in view of the position we had already taken? Russia might later demand control of the outlet from the Black Sea to the Mediterranean, a predominant position in Iran, and strategic and territorial concessions in the Far East. Would we not find it impossible to concede these claims without endangering our own security in the postwar world, and without incurring the legitimate resentment of the peoples of Turkey, the Middle East and China?

On the other hand, would not the firm rejection of Russia's claims cause a breakdown in Russian co-operation in the war against Germany or, even worse (and this possibility was uppermost in the minds of the Joint Chiefs of Staff throughout the war), encourage the Kremlin to negotiate a separate peace with Hitler? The Joint Chiefs frequently emphasized the significance of the British Cabinet's belief that a message received from Moscow as early as September 5, 1941, implied that Stalin was already thinking of separate peace terms with Germany. Such arguments as these would at any time have been persuasive. During the dark year of 1942, they proved to be decisive.

There were other considerations as well. The Secretary of

State was temperamentally disposed to put off dealing with controversial issues as long as possible. He preferred not to cross the proverbial bridge until he came to it. A remedial policy was to him preferable to a preventive policy, even though, as events so often showed, a preventive policy adopted at the psychological moment and carried out with decision and dispatch might later save a world of remedy. If the discussion of such exceedingly thorny problems at the Baltic states or Poland's eastern frontiers could be postponed until a peace conference, that was infinitely better than grasping the nettle firmly now. And this was a moment, it is to be remembered, when as a result of the extreme friction that had arisen between President Roosevelt and Mr. Hull in January, 1942, the President was making every effort to avoid decisions that ran counter to Mr. Hull's recommendations.

Nor must we lose sight of the President's preoccupation with his role as wartime leader of the American people. He was determined to preserve national unity. If it became known that the Government was discussing with other nations the future status of Poland, the future status of the Baltic states, and other East European settlements, there was little doubt that large racial minorities in this country, hearing wholly unfounded versions of the Government's decisions, would at once be greatly exercised and split into quarreling and antagonistic groups.

Last, but by no means least, was the fact that while the President clearly saw the advantages in going to the peace conference with prior agreements on political and territorial problems, he by no means felt that to postpone discussion of these issues need seriously prejudice our hope of securing a good peace. For he had, and justly, great confidence in his own ability as a negotiator.

It is perhaps only fair to add that Roosevelt was occasionally apt to rely too greatly upon a few favorite panaceas for problems that were actually too basic and far-reaching in their origins and nature to admit of any easy solutions. For example, he had faith in the efficacy of plebiscites for most of Europe's territorial controversies. He was even more wedded to the idea that plebiscites are a universal remedy than Woodrow Wilson had been. It was at about this time that he talked to me for well over an hour one evening about the desirability of using plebiscites to settle once and for all the friction between the Serbs, the Croats and the Slovenes which had so beclouded the history of Yugoslavia as an independent state. He did not apparently attribute much importance to the harm that would be done to the national economies of all three peoples should they decide to become independent entities; nor did he have much in mind the impoverishment and general misery that had spread over most of the Danube basin after the Treaty of Versailles had dissolved the Austro-Hungarian Empire and the economic federation that the Empire represented. His strong sense of justice responded instinctively to a freely held plebiscite as a means of preventing the subjugation of national minorities. But he failed fully to take into account the very practical consideration that the further fractionization he proposed would merely increase the economic maladjustments that had been one of the chief causes for Europe's woes during the years between the two World Wars.

He also intended to recommend the plebiscite principle if and when the time came to discuss the future of the Baltic states with Stalin. He said he was certain he could get Stalin to agree to a freely conducted plebiscite, under international auspices, in all three of the republics. As is now well known, the President found out at Yalta how vain this illusion had been. Stalin told him that the subject was one that he refused to discuss, since the Baltic peoples had already voted to join the Soviet Union.

Yet as the months passed, it became plain that while it might be much easier, and in some ways perhaps more expedient, to postpone such problems as these until the peace conference, the morale of certain countries, like China, would be seriously impaired if their Government could be given no firm assurances about their future status. It was also becoming more and more apparent that the appetite of a victorious Soviet Union might well become inordinate if no effort to check it was made before the end of the war.

The recognition of these imperious necessities resulted in a number of purely political declarations. A declaration covering the restoration of Austrian independence and the future status of Italy was issued when the foreign ministers of the four major allies met in Moscow in October, 1943, and another covering Korean independence, and the restoration to China of Manchuria, Formosa and the Pescadores was made when the President met with Chiang Kai-shek and Churchill at Cairo in December of the same year.

Necessity also paved the way for the agreement to establish a European Advisory Commission to consider the treatment to be accorded the European enemy states. Because a number of highly qualified advisers were appointed to the Commission, useful documentation on Europe's political and territorial problems was compiled, but the Commission itself failed during the year and a half of its existence to negotiate any political agreements of importance whatever.

At Tehran and at Yalta, new and significant political agreements were reached. It was at Tehran that the President first brought up the suggestion that Russia should have access to the Manchurian port of Dairen. It was at Tehran that Stalin temporarily reversed the position he had taken in his conferences with Eden the year before, stating that there was no need for him at that moment to speak of Russia's future territorial interests, but adding, not without grim significance, that "When the time comes we will speak." It was at Yalta that Roosevelt and Churchill conceded Stalin's Far Eastern demands covering the return of southern Sakhalin and the Kurile Islands to Russia, and a position in Manchuria that was tantamount to full control of that ancient province. At Yalta, also, the precise limits of Poland's future territory were taken up, together with the political composition of her future government.

What this brief record shows is that the position so confidently and firmly taken by the British and American governments in January, 1942, was wholly at variance with the course that they later actually pursued. This change of policy on a matter of vital significance was apparently due to no conscious decision by either of them; rather they seem to have drifted into it without any real apprehension of all its implications.

It must be ruefully admitted also that many of our discussions of postwar territorial and political problems with the Soviet Union were undertaken in a singularly haphazard fashion, and without full consideration or preparation. The United States had two clear-cut alternatives in January, 1942. One was to create the official international planning commission that Mrs. Roosevelt had suggested, in the hope that the major allies would at that crucial moment in the war be able to work out political and territorial solutions that would be found acceptable at the end of the war. The other alternative was to refuse resolutely to discuss any political or territorial question until a peace conference assembled.

Each course had its advantages and its disadvantages. My own judgment now, as it was then, is that the advantages of the former far outweighed its disadvantages. By sticking neither to one course nor the other we fell, as so often happens in such cases, between two stools. The immense influence that we possessed immediately after Pearl Harbor was not exercised. When we did attempt to negotiate political settlements, our influence was no longer decisive.

And it would be hard to deny that our influence before 1943 would probably have been conclusive if we had used it to secure postwar settlements that, while insuring legitimate security to the Russian people, would have seemed just and wise to a majority of the remaining peoples of the world. At that stage the moral influence of this country was incomparably greater than that of either of its major allies. It is true that Mr. Churchill had roused the hearts and souls of the English-speaking world by his resplendent war leadership. But the part his predecessors had played in European affairs during the decades between the two World Wars, his own more recent quarrel with the French, and Britain's role as a colonial power in Asia, Africa, and the Near East, deprived the British Government of the measure of popular confidence that the United States then enjoyed in every part of the world.

As for the Soviet Government, the suspicion and mistrust aroused by its policy after 1917, and the long war waged by the Kremlin upon organized religion, had lost for the Soviet Union the moral support of a large part of the world outside the Communist Party membership. Her struggle against Hitlerism had

regained for her a measure of the popular backing she had for-
feited. Nevertheless, it was to the United States and, in particular, to Roosevelt himself, that countless millions in every part of
the globe were turning, in the hope that American leadership
would win them freedom and security. Even within the Soviet
Union there were no few signs that the people were beginning
to realize that Roosevelt was not the pawn of Wall Street, nor a
"capitalist reactionary," but rather the spokesman for a free and
generous nation joined with them in the struggle to defeat the
invaders of "Mother Russia."

The political influence of the United States was then at its
peak. Our military strength was already far greater, in proportion
to the strength of our allies, than it had ever been during the
First World War. The success of the North African operation
was to most observers convincing evidence of the reserve power
that the United States possessed and soon would bring into play.
It is true that two years later the ground forces and the air force
were to be immeasurably greater in striking power. But by then
the Soviet armies had demonstrably defeated the Nazi invaders.

In the field of production the United States was supreme.
Stalin himself, at the Tehran Conference the end of that same
year, declared that, except for American production, "the war
would have been lost." The armament production that he wrested
from the hardly beset Russian people after the German invasion
was nothing short of miraculous. But in those first dire months
the Russian armies were so sorely pressed that he begged both
the British and American governments to send divisions under
their own command to help fight on Russian soil. And it should
never be forgotten that the arms and airplanes he received from
the then limited resources of the United States helped greatly to

make possible the victory at Moscow. What American production through Lend-Lease meant to Russia could not be better shown than in this passage from Deutscher's political biography of Stalin[3]:

The weapons which the Western powers supplied were a useful and in some cases vital addition. But the lorries which carried the Russian divisions into Germany were most of American, Canadian and British make—more than four hundred thousand lorries were supplied to Russia under Lend-Lease. So were most of the boots in which the infantry proper slogged its way to Berlin, through the mud and snow and sand of the Eastern European plains. Much of the armies' clothing and of its tinned food were supplied under Lend-Lease. One might sum up broadly that the fire-power of the Red Army was home produced, whereas the element of its mobility was largely imported.

Had the United States at the time of which we speak tried to get from Stalin a firm agreement on postwar political and territorial settlements, is it not probable that our influence would have been sufficient to have kept those settlements within bounds that a peace conference would have been disposed to accept as legitimate and fair?

To answer this question we must try to estimate what Stalin would have regarded as the irreducible minimum of his demands. We know what those demands were in December, 1941, when he presented them to Mr. Eden. At that very moment the German armies had reached a point only a few miles from Moscow. It would be logical to assume that with Russia's fortunes at their lowest ebb, Stalin was not resorting to sheer bargaining, and that he was sincere in maintaining that, if victorious, Russia could

[3] Deutscher, I., *Stalin, a Political Biography* (New York: Oxford University Press, 1949).

not accept less than the territorial security these demands represented.

Of the commitments for which Stalin then asked, the "Curzon Line" had long been regarded in the West as a legitimate boundary between Poland and Russia, for ethnic as well as strategic reasons. It was in fact a settlement voluntarily offered by Churchill and Roosevelt at the Tehran Conference later that year. It constituted a frontier which many of the more realistic Poles would have accepted, however reluctantly, if it had been combined with concessions to Poland in the form of a part of East Prussia and a part of Germany's eastern agricultural provinces.

The adjustments involving Bessarabia and Bukhovina were not a major difficulty. From the standpoint of the United States, only Stalin's demand for the permanent incorporation into the Soviet Union of the three Baltic republics would have been unacceptable.

On this point it is doubtful whether Stalin in the winter of 1943 would have proved altogether obdurate. Up to the time of the deal with Hitler, he had consistently opposed all projects for the increase of Russian territory. It is not often remembered nowadays that it was Stalin himself who went to Helsinki in 1917 to declare the independence of Finland from Russia. Time and again he had announced as his immutable policy, "Not one foot of foreign soil." In this he was, of course, repeating one of Lenin's most cherished tenets. And we find him in 1925 announcing that any effort by the Soviet Union to acquire spheres of influence abroad would be "the road to nationalism and degeneration, the road of full liquidation of the international policy of the proletariat." Until the eve of the Second World War, as far as we can tell from the documents so far made public, and from Stalin's support of Litvinoff's efforts before 1939 to stimulate "collective security," he had never wavered from that position. It is, therefore, by no means unreasonable to assume that we might have solved this one basic difficulty if we had broached the matter in the early days of the joint war effort and given him some assurance of security against a future attack by a rearmed Germany. For this danger was with him an obsession governing all his thinking in his dealings with his major allies.

What alternative did he have in the winter of 1943? He could not have run the risk of losing Lend-Lease assistance or Anglo-American co-operation without inviting a Russian defeat. The consensus in Washington and London was that he might sue for a separate peace with Germany. We now know that he was, in fact, equally fearful that his Western allies might sue for a separate peace. Yet had he done so, no step would then have been more unpopular with the Russian people, who had been aroused to savage fury by the devastation of their homeland and the atrocities of the Germans. And Stalin at that time had by no means attained the measure of popularity that was to be his during the last years of the war. Finally, there was small prospect at that moment that he could secure from an enraged Hitler peace terms even as good as those granted by the shameful peace at Brest-Litovsk twenty-five years before.

After the winter of 1943, two phenomena were to be observed. Following the victory at Stalingrad and the eventual German retreat, the Russian armies rapidly occupied the territory Stalin claimed. The moment for negotiation was gone. Simultaneously, as Russia's military strength increased, the leverage that American political, military and productive strength could exert upon the Kremlin correspondingly diminished. The Soviet Union had become the most powerful entity in Europe and in Asia, and her ambitions grew proportionately.

That these two developments should, in the light of the history of the last century, have been anticipated, now seems obvious. But knowledge of modern history has not been a forte of our more recent Secretaries of State. To those within the Government who had some familiarity with the history of Europe it seemed certainly worth bearing in mind that demands for zones of influence, for territory, and for warm-water ports had been recurrent from the time of Peter the Great, and had been pressed with peculiar vigor whenever the Russian military was in the ascendancy. They had been made even during Kerenski's short-lived liberal regime by his Foreign Minister, Professor Milyukov. They had subsequently been urged several times by important sectors of the Bolshevik regime and had been quashed only by the weight of the Lenin tradition.

One further point should not have been overlooked. The original policies of the Bolshevik revolution were dictated by Lenin, an internationalist, who had spent the better part of his life in exile. But for more than a decade the power to determine Russian destinies had been wielded by Stalin, who had scarcely ever lived outside Russia, and who had devoted much of his energy to proving that his Georgian birth did not prevent him from being Russia's foremost nationalist. If a reversal of policy became expedient, Stalin had no personal inhibitions to stand in the way. If the Russian armies now proved triumphant, it was safe to predict that the Red Army would clamor for the victor's spoils and that at the peace conference, in the absence of any prior commitments to the contrary, Stalin would find it as difficult to stand up against his marshals and generals as had Alexander I at the Congress of Vienna. Yet these simple lessons of history were generally ignored. So it happened that at the moment when the influence of the United States would have been most effective, it was not exerted.

As I see it, the critics of the agreements reached at Tehran, Yalta, and Potsdam are confusing cause and effect. The agreements so bitterly assailed would have been far different had the President decided in 1942 to insist upon the creation of a United Nations Council charged with the duty of finding solutions for political and territorial problems before the end of the war. His refusal to do so was in accord with the advice given him by his Secretary of State, the Joint Chiefs of Staff, and by most of his White House advisers, as well as with the views then held by the Prime Minister of Great Britain. It was a decision dictated by the President's conviction that as Commander-in-Chief his paramount obligation was to permit nothing to jeopardize the winning of the war. Yet with the advantage that hindsight gives us, it seems fair to say that it was this decision that was largely responsible for the division of the world today into two increasingly warring camps.

CHAPTER VI

Far Eastern Policy from
Pearl Harbor to Hiroshima

WHEN Japan's capitulation was signed on the deck of the U.S.S. *Missouri* on September 2, 1945, the United States possessed the most sweeping control over the Pacific that any power had ever been able to maintain.

In a long series of costly and bloody engagements its navy, air force and ground troops had swept the Japanese aggressors back to their home islands from the Pacific territories they had seized. By the surrender terms signed in Yokohama Bay, the Japanese divisions that had overrun so many of the Chinese provinces were committed to surrender to the forces of America's allies, China and the Soviet Union; and the Japanese troops in Southeast Asia to the United Nations armies under the command of Lord Mountbatten. All the strategic Pacific bases from the Aleutians to the Philippines were in American hands. The island of Okinawa, less than four hundred miles from Japan proper, had become an American fortress.

Japan was to be subjected to military occupation for an indefinite period. The victorious allies had agreed that the occupation should be headed by an American Commander-in-Chief, General MacArthur. The occupying forces were to be chiefly American. Responsibility for the determination of occupation policy was to be also primarily American.

In China the Nationalist Government of Generalissimo Chiang Kai-shek remained in power. There was good reason to assume that with the pledged support of the Soviet Union and of the United States it would gradually overcome the opposition of the Chinese Communists and consolidate its authority over a united nation.

In accordance with the commitments made at Cairo two years before, which promised independence and territorial integrity to the Korean people, the United Nations was to put the preliminary administration of Korea under a trusteeship of the United States, the Soviet Union, China and Great Britain, to continue only until the Korean people were prepared to resume their obligations as a sovereign nation.

While a few were questioning the wisdom of some of the Far Eastern agreements made at Yalta, those who were not motivated by purely political partisanship were generally willing to concede that, if these agreements would tend to prevent postwar controversies between the major allies, make for co-operation between Moscow and Washington, as well as between Moscow and Nanking, and promote the rapid pacification and recovery of a devastated sector of the globe, the concessions by China that they involved would be justified in China's own highest interest.

The Japanese invasion of China and of southeastern Asia had speeded the development of new forces that could no longer be checked, and that must radically change the future political structure of Asia. The swift rise of nationalism throughout the Asiatic world from India and Indonesia, through Burma and Malaya, to Indo-China and China herself was an unmistakable sign that

Finis must now be written to the history of Western imperialism in the Far East. It was confidently expected that through the means provided by the Charter of the United Nations the peoples clamoring for freedom could be helped by the older countries, and particularly by the United States, to assume rapidly the responsibilities of independence. Thereby they would be spared many of the birth pangs that have so often attended the emergence to liberty of subjugated races.

No reasonable man could have been so ingenuous as to assume in September, 1945, that the infinitely complicated machinery of rehabilitation was going to function smoothly without many a breakdown. Yet he would have seemed to be equally unrealistic had he anticipated all that has since taken place.

As these lines are written, exactly five years after the ceremony on the deck of the U.S.S. *Missouri*, American troops, acting under the authority of the United Nations, are waging a desperate struggle to repel a Soviet-inspired and Chinese-Communist–abetted invasion of the Republic of South Korea, created and recognized by the United Nations.

All the mainland of China is under the control of a Chinese Communist government notoriously hostile to the United States. Chiang Kai-shek's Nationalist Government has taken refuge on the island of Formosa, which the United States has declared it will help to defend, but whose ultimate disposition must be determined by the United Nations. It is increasingly probable that the United States may be drawn into war with Communist China.

Washington is offering such assistance as it can to the non-Communist governments of Indo-China, Indonesia, Burma and Malaya.

Tibet has been invaded by the Chinese Communists. In India,

in Pakistan, and in the Philippines the probability of Communist uprisings is admitted.

By its amazingly effective use of the "big lie" tactics that Hitler so successfully employed, Soviet propaganda has already aroused throughout Asia much animosity against the United States and suspicion of our ulterior purposes. Moscow is using the Security Council of the United Nations as a forum from which to make it appear that truth is falsehood, and that the aggression against the Korean people was ordered not by Stalin but by Truman. The Asiatic peoples are being told that it is not Russia that is preventing the unification of Korea, and the re-establishment of Korean independence, but the "warmongers of Wall Street."

Asia is seething from one end to the other with panic fear. Except for Japan there is no Asiatic country where starvation, misery and suffering are not more prevalent today than they were five years ago.

Now, why did all this happen?

Is it all due, as the more virulent of President Roosevelt's critics tell us, to his incapacity and illness, to his efforts to "appease" Russia, and to the decisions he made at Cairo, Tehran and Yalta?

Is it due to the foreign policy, and in particular to the Far Eastern policy, pursued by the United States since the death of President Roosevelt?

Is it due to a spontaneous transformation of Soviet world policy since the spring of 1945?

Or is it due perhaps to a combination of the two latter factors, and to acts of omission and of commission for which both the United States and the Soviet Union have been responsible since as well as during the Second World War?

It may be useful on this tragic anniversary to review the record of these past years, and to seek to distinguish facts from myths or vicious fabrications.

I will take as a starting point a talk that I had with President Roosevelt when I was his guest at Hyde Park one Sunday late in September, 1943.

The President had also staying with him for the week end the Crown Princess of Norway and her children, her lady- and gentleman-in-waiting, as well as his youngest son and the latter's wife. It was one of those gleaming autumn days that the Hudson River Valley knows so well. We had all had lunch at the President's hilltop cottage. Afterward the President had driven me back to the "Big House," and had taken me into the tiny study where he loved to work, and from which he so often broadcast to the nation. In the course of a conversation that ranged over a multitude of issues he turned to the Far East. After going into the military situation in some detail, he spoke of the political and territorial readjustments that should be made after the war.

He dealt for a while with one of his favorite projects, the severance of Indo-China from French control, and the establishment there of a United Nations trusteeship in which the Philippines should play a prominent part. As a result of his talks with Queen Wilhelmina of the Netherlands and with members of the Dutch Government, he felt that the Dutch would be able after the war to work out a satisfactory solution for the Netherlands East Indies; one which would give the Indonesian people full partnership in a Netherlands federation. He referred ruefully to Mr. Churchill's stubborn opposition to the suggestions that he had offered to expedite a dominion status for India. But he expressed the firm conviction that as soon as the war was over the peoples of India, either as a unit or after partition, would achieve full self-government.

To the President, of course, the key to the Far Eastern puzzle was China. I need not here elaborate on what I have already emphasized in a previous chapter, his peculiarly friendly regard for the Chinese people, and his belief that American foreign policy in the Far East should be predicated upon a close working relation between the Chinese and American governments. He told me of the innumerable difficulties he had recently been having with Chiang Kai-shek, whom he classified as "highly temperamental." He spoke in no measured terms of the corruption and inefficiency which characterized his administration. He had no patience with the regime's apparent lack of sympathy for the abject misery of the masses of the Chinese people. But he recognized as valid the reasons for its very natural resentment at the meager assistance we were at that moment able to provide, and its irritation at seeing desperately needed matériel frequently diverted to the British. He felt, he said, that the Generalissimo, limited as his military vision might be, and badly as his troops were fighting, was the only Chinese leader who could keep the Chinese armies in the field against the Japanese and who would be able after the war to hold the Chinese people together. He added that the services he had already rendered China were incalculable. He was worried lest the Soviet Government now give overt help to the factions opposing the Nationalist armies. For that reason he was anxious to see us do everything we could to compose the differences between Chungking and the Communists, in order that Chiang could continue fighting the Japanese, and not have to expend the ebbing strength of his troops in fighting other Chinese.

But what he feared most of all was the flaring up of civil war in China after Japan's defeat. The danger there was that the Soviet Union would intervene in behalf of the Communists, and the Western powers would be tempted or forced in their own interest to back the anti-Communist side. We would then see, he said, very much the same situation that we had witnessed in Spain during her civil war, only on a far greater scale, and with graver dangers inherent in it. It was his thought that no spot was more likely to create difficulties in the postwar years than China, unless she could be rapidly helped by the outside world to restore her national economy and to repair some of the damage done by the long years of Japanese aggression. She would also need a firm agreement with Moscow that would prevent the kind of Soviet interference in her internal affairs that had existed continuously after the First World War.

I reminded the President of the talks we had had the spring before with Madame Chiang Kai-shek when she had come to Washington. He had then assured her of his own agreement with the position of the Nationalist Government, that no Far Eastern readjustment could be stable or lasting unless China got back not only the territory that Japan had seized, but also the territories taken from her in preceding generations by other foreign powers, including Hongkong.

The President said he of course remained of the same mind. He realized, however, how difficult it was going to be to convince Mr. Churchill, or for that matter any British Government, that after a war in which Britain had been one of the victorious allies, she should be deprived by the peace treaty of a colony she had held for a century. As for Formosa, he said it should be returned to China; but this arrangement must include the establishment there of a strategic air base for the use of the United Nations police force. He stressed especially the strategic importance of Formosa in enforcing peace in the Pacific.

I remember very clearly asking at that juncture if he was not afraid that the Russians would put in a claim for the concessions they had wrested from China during the final years of the tottering Chinese Empire, and which Japan had later taken over, as well as for the territories they had ceded to Japan after their defeat in 1905.

The President answered that, while he thought the Russians should, of course, get back the Kurile Islands and southern Sakhalin, ceded under the Treaty of Portsmouth, he was hopeful that they would not claim more than legitimate trade facilities in Manchuria. He was thinking of suggesting that Dairen be made a free port to satisfy them on that issue. (The establishment of free ports in many parts of the world, and particularly in localities such as Kiel where international controversies threatened to arise, was always one of President Roosevelt's favorite formulas. In the case of Dairen, it will be remembered that this was precisely what he proposed to Stalin a few months later at Tehran.)

We did not touch upon the question of Korea at that time. But we had discussed it in several talks earlier that summer, and the President had then expressed the view that Korea should be reconstituted as an independent republic under a preliminary trusteeship composed of China, the Soviet Union, Great Britain, the United States and Canada.

The record of our conversation of September, 1943, shows in

considerable detail precisely what President Roosevelt was then thinking about postwar settlements in the Far East. American influence should be exerted to attain these objectives:

1. The restoration to China of all territory previously taken from her by conquest, or by coercion.

2. Support for the Chinese Nationalist Government as the only regime capable of unifying China and of preventing a long drawn-out civil war.

3. An agreement between China and the Soviet Union which would preclude Soviet interference in China's internal affairs or encroachment upon Chinese territory.

In my next conversation with the President, which took place at the White House a month later, just before he left for Cairo and Tehran, the President mentioned the trouble he had been having in convincing Mr. Churchill that China should be treated as one of the four major powers. He said he had told the Prime Minister that if the major allies were going to undertake the task of keeping peace after the war China should be associated with them.

Mr. Churchill's view, he told me, was that the job should be done solely by the English-speaking powers. He was willing, even though reluctant, to concede that Russia might have to become a partner in the enterprise. The President had the idea that Mr. Churchill's thinking was governed by his unwillingness to see that the British Empire as it had existed at the turn of the century was long since a thing of the past. He himself was persuaded that the Western world, for its own safety's sake, must abandon once and for all the idea that the Asiatic peoples were inferior races, and must work wholeheartedly with China from the outset as the best means of preventing a fundamental cleavage between the West and the East in the years to come.

I have not found in the records of any of the negotiations or international conferences in which the President took part any evidence that he himself ever swerved from the general objectives that he thus outlined to me.

It is true that friction between the President and Chiang Kai-shek's Government periodically became acute. Specific pledges of military assistance were sometimes not kept, as when Roosevelt reversed his previous commitment to occupy the Andaman Islands as a part of the Burma campaign. The violent feud between General Stillwell and the Generalissimo gave rise to deep resentment in Chungking, just as the Generalissimo's repeated refusal to abide by American advice on strategy and personnel aroused equal resentment in Washington. The repeated—and, it must be admitted, bungling—efforts of several of President Roose-velt's representatives in China to persuade Chiang Kai-shek to comply with the demands of the Chinese Communists were productive of misunderstanding, and damaged the prestige and authority of the Nationalist Government.

Likewise the profound ignorance of China, and the lack of Far Eastern experience, of certain of the President's representatives there served him in ill stead. These envoys spent much of their time quarreling with each other, or with their subordinates; and, while I know of no instance where they did not try to carry out the President's instructions to further the establishment of a strong postwar China, their erroneous judgment and the wide diversity of their recommendations made it impossible for him to obtain any accurate over-all estimate of the situation.

So badly did these envoys inform the President that he could express the opinion to Stalin at Yalta that, in the light of the information he had received from his latest batch of representatives in Chungking, the responsibility for the refusal of the Chinese Communists to co-operate with the Nationalist Government lay with the Comintern and the Kuomintang rather than with the Chinese Communists themselves. Yet despite the inaccurate information he received, the President neither modified the policy upon which he had embarked nor changed his original objective of a strong and united postwar China.

From first to last the support given by Roosevelt to the Nationalist Government of China was unwavering. The amount of military, and, even more, of material assistance granted under the President's direction was enormous.

The crux of the charges leveled against Roosevelt's Far Eastern policy is to be found in the charge that by the agreements he made with Stalin at Yalta, China was "sold out" and our own strategic position gravely impaired. Let us see just how much justification there is for this.

First in January, 1943, and again in October of the same year Stalin formally committed Russia to join the war against Japan after Germany's defeat. Those assurances were repeated to the American Ambassador in Moscow in October, 1944.

In the earlier stages of the war we were faced with the prospect of a long drawn-out and grueling struggle to win back by our own, almost unaided, efforts the control of the Pacific. At that time, the assistance that Russia could have given us, had it been feasible, would have been deemed invaluable.

By the autumn of 1944, however, some of the President's ablest staff advisers had reached a far different conclusion. To them

Japan was already to all intents and purposes defeated. The naval and air blockade of Japan was nearly complete. Its continuation must sooner or later bring about her submission, without any need for an American invasion of her home islands.

These advisers, and among them Admiral Leahy was outstanding, proposed that the United States should limit itself to continuing the naval and air blockade of Japan, occupying the Philippines and perhaps a number of strategic points on the coast of the mainland of China.

The Army, on the other hand, speaking through the Chief of Staff, General Marshall, insisted that Japan could be compelled to surrender only by a progressive occupation of her main islands, commencing with an American amphibious invasion of the southern island of Kyushu.

This fundamental difference in the strategic advice given to the President first became acute immediately before the second conference at Quebec, which President Roosevelt held with Mr. Churchill in September, 1944. At Quebec, after full debate, the Combined Chiefs of Staff of the United States and of Great Britain recommended that, once Germany was defeated, the two countries, *together with Russia*, throw all their available resources into the battle against Japan. They fixed as the time for a probable final victory over Japan a date approximately eighteen months after Germany's defeat. The advice of Admiral Leahy, and of those who held with him, was disregarded by the Combined Chiefs.

The alternatives before the President were therefore these: to adopt or not to adopt the recommendation of the Combined Chiefs of Staff. Their advice represented the considered decision of the heads of the American and British armies, including General Marshall, whose strategy had consistently proved to be brilliantly successful throughout the North African and European campaigns. Though it envisaged the loss of many thousands of American lives during the invasion of the Japanese homeland, it was the strategy believed to be essential to defeat Japan at the earliest possible moment.

We now know from the evidence produced before the War Crimes Tribunal at Tokyo, and also from the testimony of competent officials who held office in the Japanese Government during the war years, that the advice given by Admiral Leahy and those who agreed with him was sound, and that Japan could not have held out for long even in the absence of an invasion. The recommendation of the Combined Chiefs was offered under a basic misapprehension of existing facts. Yet upon a question such as this, which was almost entirely one of technical military strategy, would the President have been warranted in disregarding the recommendations formally submitted to him and to Mr. Churchill by the Combined Chiefs of Staff of the two governments?

Once the President's decision had been made, it necessarily became the foundation for the military and political planning at the Yalta Conference a few months later. And it was the President's highest obligation to take every possible step to ensure the success of the operation and to keep to a minimum the loss of American lives. His military advisers insisted that for this we must have Russian help, including not only the use of Russian divisions against the Japanese armies in Manchuria, but also the use of Russian territory for American air force bases.

At Yalta President Roosevelt told Stalin that, while he hoped the invasion of Japan might yet be found unnecessary, she still had some four million men under arms, and without intensified bombing her defeat could not be foreseen. He asked that for that purpose we be granted bases on Russian soil. Stalin authorized the establishment of American air bases at Komsomolsk and Nikolaevsk, and expressed no objection to the establishment of additional bases in Russia's maritime provinces.

In a private conference with the President, Stalin then made known Russia's Far Eastern demands: The Soviet Union wished to obtain from China a long-term lease of Port Arthur, the establishment of Dairen as a free port, a lease of the Chinese Manchurian railroads, and her agreement to the continued autonomy of Outer Mongolia, as well as to the cession to Russia of the Japanese-held Sakhalin and Kurile Islands. Stalin maintained, as he repeated to Harry Hopkins six months later at Moscow, that after the sufferings they had already experienced the Russian people must be given "a good reason for going to war against Japan." He stated that a guaranty by the United States and Great Britain that China would grant these demands must be a prerequisite of Russian participation in the war. The President, and subsequently Mr. Churchill, agreed to these conditions.

It is this agreement which, it is charged by the President's critics, "sold China down the river," and fatally undermined our own strategic position in the Far East.

Of such critics Mr. Hanson W. Baldwin, the military expert of the *New York Times,* is surely among the most authoritative and reputable. In his book *Great Mistakes of the War*[1] he says that at Yalta

. . . the United States representatives placed themselves in the

[1] Baldwin, Hanson W., *Great Mistakes of the War* (New York: Harper & Brothers, 1950), p. 777.

amazing position of "giving away" territories which did not belong to us, and of undertaking to secure concessions which impaired the sovereignty of a friendly allied state. The political misconception, so obvious now, should have been apparent then; it was not to our interest, or the interests of China or of the world, to make Russia a Pacific power; it was not to our interest to beg or borrow for Russia's entry into the Pacific war.

Nor should military considerations have affected this political judgment. At the time of Yalta, Japan was already beaten—not by the atomic bomb which had not yet been perfected, not by conventional bombing, then just starting, but by attrition and blockade. . . . The full seriousness of the Japanese plight was not then, of course, completely understood. Our military men were preoccupied and concerned with the fierceness of the Japanese defense: the tactical situation obscured the hopeless strategic position of Japan, and some of our Commanders took, therefore, far too pessimistic a view.

In his summary Mr. Baldwin concludes:

Russia drove a hard bargain at Yalta. Stalin promised to enter the war against Japan within an estimated ninety days after the end of the war against Germany, but for it he got the Kurile Islands, all of Sakhalin, a half interest in the railways in Manchuria, Port Arthur, a Russian-controlled "free port" in Dairen, and thus strategic hegemony in important Northeast Asia.

There can be no quarrel today with Mr. Baldwin's assertion that at the second conference at Quebec and at the Yalta conference the Combined Chiefs of Staff were guilty of a "fundamental military misconception." But one may legitimately wonder whether Mr. Baldwin would maintain that, if Russia had not joined in the war against Japan, Stalin would have been thereby prevented from making these claims. In 1945 peoples everywhere believed that the only hope for future peace lay in co-operation between the Soviet Union and the West. The Russian territorial claims were widely regarded as being legitimate and just. Is it probable, once these claims were entered by Stalin at a peace conference, that the United States and Britain could have successfully rejected them?

What I chiefly question is the validity of Mr. Baldwin's further assertion that President Roosevelt's acquiescence in Stalin's demands involved a "fundamental political misconception."

This is the complaint voiced by the four Republican Senators on the Foreign Relations Committee in August, 1950. They declared that, "The major tragedy of our time was the failure and refusal of American leadership in 1945 to recognize the true aims and methods of the rulers of Soviet Russia."

As I have endeavored to show, in his approach to Far Eastern postwar settlements President Roosevelt was guided by the conviction that our interests, the interests of China and of the world, would best be served by the unification of the Chinese people and the creation of a strong postwar China. He held that the best assurance of this would be a firm agreement between Moscow and the Chinese Nationalist Government guaranteeing Stalin's support of the Government of Chiang Kai-shek and his noninterference in China's internal affairs.

Those who condemn the policy for which that conviction was responsible now maintain that the hope for Chinese unification was wholly illusory, and that Mr. Churchill's opposition to the recognition of China as a major power was altogether justified.

What, in 1945, would the alternatives to that policy have been?

Had the Chinese people been summarily dismissed as a potentially constructive force in Asia, to welter indefinitely in civil

war and anarchy, what other power could have counterbalanced
the weight of the Soviet Union in the Far East? The Allies were
pledged to disarm and to demilitarize Japan. The Island Empire
was to become a Far Eastern Switzerland. No sane statesman
would at that time have considered the suggestion that immediately after Japan's defeat she should instantly be rearmed in order
to prevent Russia from moving into the vacuum to be created
by a decision to leave China inert and impotent.

I can see no alternative to the policy decided upon by the
President which in 1945 would have seemed to promise so much
hope for success in the construction of a péaceful Asia.

Four years ago I expressed the view[2] that

Russian possession of southern Sakhalin and of the Kuriles is
essential if the Soviet Government is to obtain security for its Siberian
provinces. Both territories were torn from Russia by Japan. The inter-
nationalization of Dairen and the grant of permanent autonomy to
Outer Mongolia have a considerable measure of justification. However, the restoration to Russia of the right formerly possessed by the
Imperial Russian Governments to dominate Manchuria through the
control of the Chinese Eastern and South Manchurian Railroads,
and the lease of Port Arthur as a naval base necessarily fall into a
different category. These concessions, which will make it altogether
impossible for a new unified China to exercise full sovereignty within
Manchuria, are all the more objectionable in view of China's absence
from the conference table when they were decided.

I have not modified that opinion.

Nevertheless, if Stalin had respected the treaty with the Chinese Nationalist Government which he signed at Moscow in
June, 1945, and which embodied the Yalta agreements, that

---

[2] Welles, Sumner, *Where Are We Heading?* (New York: Harper &
Brothers, 1946), p. 299.

treaty would have paved the way for the unification of China and for the eventual creation of a strong postwar China.

It may be recalled that when Harry Hopkins was sent by President Truman to Moscow six months after the Yalta agreements were signed, he cabled this report to Washington:

[Stalin] made categorical statement that he would do everything he could to promote unification of China under the leadership of Chiang Kai-shek. He further stated that this leadership should continue after the war because no one else was strong enough. He specifically stated that no Communist leader was strong enough to unify China. . . . Stalin repeated all of his statements made at Yalta, that he wanted a unified and stable China and wanted China to control all of Manchuria as part of a united China. . . . He agreed with America's "open door" policy and went out of his way to indicate that the United States was the only power with the resources to aid China economically after the war. He observed that for many years to come Russia would have all it could do to provide for the internal economy of the Soviet Union.

What to me is the most remarkable feature of Mr. Baldwin's criticism of the Yalta Agreement is the implication which must be drawn from the paragraphs I have quoted from his book that President Roosevelt had the authority at Yalta to determine whether or not "to make Russia a Pacific power." Russia had already for a century been a leading Pacific power. It was inconceivable in 1945 that a victorious Soviet Union would meekly resign herself at the peace conference to a denial of her claim for the return of territory earlier taken from her by a defeated Japan.

It was inconceivable that her agreement to respect China's independence and integrity and to promote the unification of China under the Chinese Nationalist Government, which the President regarded as essential to China's future safety, could be secured were the United States to refuse to agree to the return of that territory.

It was inconceivable that we could enlist her co-operation within the United Nations, or in the stabilization of Europe and of the Far East if we refused to admit her traditional position as a Pacific power on the ground that this "was not to our interest."

It was inconceivable in 1945 that American or Western European public opinion, then so eagerly hoping that co-operation with the Soviet Union might prove possible, would have supported any such policy on the part of the United States.

Much as I regret Roosevelt's belief that it was imperative for him to acquiesce in Stalin's demands regarding Manchuria, I am fully convinced that the military exigencies he believed then existed, on the report of the Combined Chiefs of Staff, and the advantages to China that he thought would come from a firm agreement with the Soviet Union, justified the decision he made.

The best answer to Mr. Baldwin and to his fellow critics of the Far Eastern agreement signed at Yalta is in these lapidary sentences of Admiral Leahy[3]:

1. Russia was our ally, and up to June, 1944, took the full force of the mighty German Army.

2. Fears expressed by many, some in high places, that Russia would make a separate peace with Germany, particularly when we were unable to mount a second front in 1943, had proved unfounded. Russia had kept every military agreement made before that time.

3. As for political agreements, we had reached at Yalta the first major understanding regarding the postwar world. Russia had shown a conciliatory attitude on the United Nations, on giving France a voice in the control council of Germany, and in agreeing to reorgani-

[3] Leahy, William, *I Was There* (New York: McGraw Hill Book Co., Inc., 1950), p. 317.

zation of the Polish and Yugoslav Governments. In fact, on almost every political problem, after a forceful statement of their views, the Russians had made sufficient concessions for an agreement to be reached, on paper at least.

In view of Russia's record during the war, was there any reason why President Roosevelt should have assumed that the Yalta agreements would be reached only "on paper"?

In the search for the answer to the fundamental question posed at the beginning of this chapter, a series of facts may here be cited to throw light upon the reasons why our relations with the Soviet Union have grown progressively worse since the spring of 1945, and why the United States now faces the present desperate situation in the Far East.

When President Roosevelt returned from Yalta, he said that Stalin's position of supremacy seemed to have changed materially since the conference at Tehran. At Tehran Stalin had appeared to make decisions without hesitation, and with no indication that he needed to consult with any other Russian authorities. At Yalta President Roosevelt felt that this was no longer the case. He had the feeling that the leaders of the Red Army had become far more influential.

It is certainly true that from that time on there were many signs that Stalin's policy was designed to curry favor with the regenerated and transformed Red Army. He himself assumed the titles of Marshal and Generalissimo. Military decorations were established, and given the names of the greatest generals of the Czarist days. The military ranks and disciplines of the Imperial Russian Armies were reinstituted. Above all, Stalin inaugurated a foreign policy that was conceived in the traditional imperialistic spirit of the Czars.

The wording of his proclamation to the Russian people on August 16, 1945, announcing Japan's surrender confirmed his statement to Harry Hopkins, "that the Russian people must have a good reason for going to war." But also it was patently designed to cater to Red Army aspirations. "The defeat of Russian troops in 1904," said Stalin, "left bitter memories in the mind of the people. It lay like a black spot on our country. Our people believed and hoped that a day would come when Japan would be smashed and that blot effaced. Forty years have we, the people of the old generation, waited for this day."

So grossly does this differ from the classic Bolshevik position laid down by Lenin, who had said that the Russian defeat in 1904 gave the proletariat "reasons to rejoice" and meant that "Russian freedom has come nearer," that it is hard to believe Stalin's proclamation would have been so worded if he had not thought that such a fundamental change in Soviet policy was imperative if a split between the regime and the Red Army were to be avoided.

On reading the very detailed record which Harry Hopkins kept of his talks with Stalin in June, 1945, one is struck by the extent to which the views Stalin then expressed are surcharged by the professional military point of view. One must also be impressed by the ominous indications of growing fear and suspicion of the West throughout the series of bitter complaints that Stalin voiced against Great Britain and the United States. They were a warning signal—which was disregarded by Washington. Little, if any, effort was made by London or Washington, either before or at Potsdam, to find a constructive solution for the chief points of difference and to remove all grounds for possible later dissension between the Soviet Union and the Western powers.

Had the new American President or the new British Prime Minister possessed the measure of vision which was then so needed, they would, for example, have foreseen that the division of Korea into Russian and American zones could not fail to create serious difficulties before long.

Stalin had agreed that the trusteeship for Korea should be held by the United States, the Soviet Union, China and Great Britain. He had also expressed his approval of President Roosevelt's proposal that no foreign troops should be stationed in Korea after the defeat and withdrawal of the Japanese invaders. But during the months between the defeat of Germany and the surrender of Japan the State Department, with an almost incomprehensible lack of foresight, in view of the all too evident danger that Korea might become a bone of contention unless detailed agreements were reached before V-J Day, failed to see to it that such an agreement was concluded.

Later, when the Japanese armies were ready to surrender, the War Department in Washington realized that something must be done. Some subordinate officers in the Pentagon hastily recommended that the Russians accept the Japanese surrender north of the 38th parallel in Korea, while the American troops would accept it south of that line. I am told that this line was fixed because it seemed "convenient." Certainly it was fixed by officials with no knowledge of what they were doing, and without consulting any responsible members of the Administration who might have had some regard for the political and economic considerations which the decision so lamentably ignores.

It is important to remember that this step was not taken upon the initiative of the Soviet Union. The mistake might well have been corrected by prompt remedial action. Yet neither the White

House, the State Department nor the War Department moved until it was far too late. The artificial frontier thus set up in Korea rapidly became, as was only to be expected in view of the constantly growing antagonism between the Soviet Union and the United States, an impermeable barrier. By 1946 a familiar "People's Republic" had been set up in the north by the Red Army operating through Korean Communist stooges.

In South Korea the record of American administration is not pleasant to contemplate. The free political system we tried to set up was a deplorable failure. Even had the Koreans placed at the head of the South Korean Government been the ablest statesmen that the Far East has produced—which they certainly were not—they could not possibly have succeeded in giving their countrymen peace and prosperity in the face of the difficulties they encountered. They were not given efficient American co-operation. They were not given adequate arms for self-defense or even for the preservation of internal order. They had no encouragement to carry out the radical and far-reaching reforms that the South Korean people demanded. They were constantly frustrated by the propaganda and subversive tactics of the North Korean Communists.

What those who were then directing our foreign policy fatally ignored was that Korea is of basic significance to China. The control of Korea by any power that may menace the independence of China is a vital danger to the Chinese people. The United States should have foreseen that the agreement upon a trusteeship for Korea, in which China would participate, was of the utmost urgency if China were to be saved from Communist domination.

This is not the place to discuss the amazing anomalies and vagaries of American policy toward China since 1945. But once it was clear—and it was surely clear long before 1948 to all who wished to see—that Stalin was violating his treaty of 1945 with Chiang Kai-shek, and disregarding his pledges to the United States to support the unification of China under the Chinese Nationalist Government, the imminence of acute danger in Korea was apparent.

Just as Japan violated her solemn obligations to the League of Nations when she refused to permit League authorities to visit the Japanese mandated islands of the Pacific, so the Soviet Union violated its obligations to the United Nations when her puppet government of North Korea refused to permit a United Nations committee to visit the territory under its control.

Once Moscow had taken that step, our failure to take precautionary measures to defend South Korea against aggression from the north can hardly be understood, let alone condoned. If ever a preventive policy was called for, it was called for in this instance. Yet not only were no precautionary measures taken, but official statements were issued in Washington as late as January, 1950, from which the only inference to be drawn was that the United States would not lift a finger to prevent aggression against South Korea.

In view of its consistent inconsistency it is difficult even for the least prejudiced observer, to guess what present American foreign policy in the Far East may be. It would seem to be predicated upon the need for the rapid reconstruction of Japan as a major power to serve as a counterweight to the Soviet Union in the Far East—although the perilous uncertainties in such a policy are glaringly apparent. But whatever it is, or is not, it is certainly not the policy of Franklin Roosevelt. His policy was to make China united and strong so that neither the Soviet Union nor any other alien power could dominate her. His policy was to achieve that objective by supporting the Nationalist Government of Chiang Kai-shek. That policy, since his death, has never been wholeheartedly pursued. It was essentially scrapped by the present Administration before the autumn of 1946. It was finally relegated to limbo when General Marshall, as Secretary of State in 1947, overruled General Wedemeyer's recommendation that the United States give all-out support to the Chiang Kai-shek Government.

It is hardly logical for the critics to allege that the Roosevelt policy has failed when it has never been given a fair trial.

If the time ever comes when international controversy is less rife, and when partisan passions here at home have cooled, the objective historian will, I believe, find that the agreement Roosevelt reached at Yalta with Stalin and Churchill upon a postwar Far Eastern settlement was warranted in the light of existing conditions. The President could not then know that his military advisers were wrong and that Japan would surrender without an American invasion. He could not know that the co-operative relationship with Stalin that he had established would break down almost immediately after his death. In the winter of 1945 he hoped, as did Winston Churchill, that the Soviet Government would stand to its obligations, as it had throughout the war years. He could not know that Soviet policy would suffer a radical transformation.

It was his decision that China should be the keystone in the arch of a new Asia. To him, the best way to get a unified and strong postwar China was to do what we could to support the Nationalist Government and to make sure that all foreign powers respected her independence and integrity, in entire harmony with our traditional Open Door policy.

It has been the reversal of that decision that has so greatly contributed to the disastrous course of events in the Far East during the past four years.

CHAPTER VII

The United Nations Is Created
before the War's End

ONE man, and one man alone, made it possible for us to have a working United Nations organization before the end of the Second World War. That man was Franklin Roosevelt.

Of the two other leaders of the Grand Alliance, Churchill had been a staunch supporter of the League of Nations. But he did not believe the Second World War offered a propitious opportunity to reconstruct a federated world organization. In public statements as well as in his confidential interchanges with the President, he repeatedly insisted that it would be better to start by building up purely regional organizations which could collaborate if need arose, but which should remain autonomous for an indefinite time, or at least until it was clear whether a supreme international authority could be successfully set up over them.

Stalin, as is well known, wanted no universal organization of any kind. What he seemed at first to favor was essentially a continuing military alliance of the United States, Great Britain and the Soviet Union which would assume the right to determine the fate of all other peoples.

The intermediary and smaller nations were incapable of taking any initiative. Many of those in Europe were occupied by Germany, and their governments were in exile. No one could foresee what the peoples of these countries would want when the war was over.

Public opinion in Great Britain and in other nations of the British Commonwealth was at best lukewarm. The faith that had been placed in the League of Nations had been shattered after Munich.

Here in the United States public opinion was as yet by no means united in the belief that a new international organization was imperatively required. The early Fulbright resolution, as well as the later resolutions adopted by the Congress, had done much to make Americans realize that the victory would be but half won unless it brought with it a stable peace such as only international organization could provide. But many potent voices still preached the old delusion of isolation, and they still met with considerable popular response.

It was Roosevelt who provided the indispensable leadership. Counter to his previous inclinations, he came to the decision, even before the outcome of the war was finally certain, that the best chance for a new and better order lay in establishing a universal international organization while the major allies were still bound together in the common war effort. Thereafter, he never relaxed his efforts until he had persuaded Churchill and Stalin to support it.

What John Gunther recently wrote[1] is wholly true:

Roosevelt considered, in fact, that the stiffest fight of his entire career would be to get the Senate to ratify American participation in the new world organization. . . . He was wrong; there was very little fight. But a principal reason for this was the work he did while

[1] Gunther, John, *Roosevelt in Retrospect* (New York: Harper & Brothers, 1950), p. 328.

the war was still being fought; if he had waited, it might have been a different story. San Francisco, he told one interviewer, was the crowning act of his whole life; full, forceful, and constructive American adhesion to the new peace structure was his dearest wish. . . .

From mid-1944 on F.D.R. paid, in blunt truth, comparatively little attention to military matters; Eisenhower and other witnesses testify that the Commander-in-Chief was much more interested in post-war problems than the war itself. Yalta, and to a lesser extent Tehran, were peace as well as war conferences, and Roosevelt was actually a post-war President, even though he died before the war was over.

It was owing solely to the President's insistence, to his untiring efforts, and to the influence that he could exert upon our allies, that a United Nations Charter came into being in San Francisco two months after his death.

There is no need here to enter into any elaborate discussion of the merits or defects of the organization that the United Nations Charter set up. It is true that Russia's use of the veto from the very outset, and her more recent maneuvers to prevent the Security Council from functioning at all, have crippled the organization as it was originally conceived. Yet even so, the United Nations has been able to take far more vigorous and effective action against aggression and to further world recovery than the League of Nations could in the very heyday of its existence.

In these first years of its brief life the United Nations has been able, as in the case of Iran, to prevent the outbreak of war. When Soviet-inspired armed aggression finally took place, as in the case of Korea, the United Nations instantly interposed armed opposition. It has unified fifty-three countries in forceful resistance to aggression as they were never unified when Japan invaded China, or Italy Ethiopia.

It has been charged that the Soviet Government has used the

forum of the Security Council and of the General Assembly to put out propaganda favorable to its own ends. Yet how much greater an advantage that forum gives the fifty-three countries opposed to the Soviet Union, especially the United States, in the chance to show up instantly and effectively the hypocrisy and falsehoods of the spokesmen for Russia. If the free countries had had such a forum between 1933 and 1939, Hitler would have been hard put to it to delude the peoples of the world about his real purpose.

We know what the Kremlin's purpose now is. Knowing that, what can we think the position of the United States would be today if the United Nations had not given us the chance to unify and to rally world public opinion in opposition to Communist imperialism?

Weak and deficient as the United Nations may often have seemed to those who judge only by immediate results, it remains humanity's one great hope for a better world of the future.

As late as August, 1941, at the Atlantic Charter meeting, the President had told me that in his judgment no world organization should again be set up until the great powers had had a chance to complete a world-policing job. At the same meeting he rejected Mr. Churchill's suggestion that Great Britain and the United States jointly declare their intention to support some kind of "effective international organization" after the contest was won.

As Mr. Churchill cabled at that time to Mr. Attlee, then Lord Privy Seal[2]: "The President undoubtedly contemplates the disarmament of the guilty nations, coupled with the maintenance of strong united British and American armaments both by sea and air for a long indefinite period."

[2] Churchill, Winston, *The Grand Alliance* (Boston: Houghton Mifflin Co., 1950), p. 441.

How did it come about that within two years the President so radically modified these views that he was prepared at the Tehran conference in 1943 to initiate the negotiations with Churchill and Stalin that later made possible the Charter of San Francisco?

Many of the books that have been written about the President in the past few years and many of the official records that have now been made public here and there throw some light on the reasons. Yet I think a more comprehensible explanation is warranted.

The President's change of heart on this great issue was not due to any overnight conversion. Things rarely happened that way with him. It was attributable to a number of factors, some of them remote, and more of them immediate. To appreciate their significance, we must first understand why Roosevelt believed, as late as 1941, that the United States should make no commitment to help to rebuild an "effective international organization." What made him feel that way?

As a vice-presidential nominee in the campaign of 1920, he had made more than 800 speeches in support of the League of Nations. Yet all his intimates knew that during the following two decades his enthusiasm for the League had cooled to a point where it might fairly be described as glacial. This was owing in part, I think, to his disgust with the way in which, after the first few years of the League's existence, the British and the French, particularly the former, so frequently prevented it from facing any major issue squarely. He saw, altogether objectively, that Great Britain had consistently sought to use the League as an instrument of her own national policy, and that in more recent years the Baldwin and MacDonald Cabinets equally had prevented it from carrying out any of its imperative obligations whenever they involved British commitments that might be unpopular at home and hence politically inexpedient. He said to me once, in 1935, "The League of Nations has become nothing more than a debating society, and a poor one at that!"

It must also be remembered that the President himself, consummate politician that he was, was never blind to what was politically inexpedient. In the early thirties he felt that the American people were firmly wedded to a policy of isolation, and that the question of American participation in the League—as distinguished from the World Court—had become altogether academic. If he had raised the League issue in the campaigns of 1932 or 1936, his Republican opponents, he knew, would have secured great political advantage from playing again on all the jealousies, fears and suspicions that had so fatally confused the voters in the 1920 campaign.

It is also, perhaps, characteristic of many of the members of the Roosevelt clan to overestimate the inherent value of success and to appraise unsuccessful causes and endeavors too cheaply merely because of their failure. And no one could deny that in its final stage the League of Nations had been an abject failure.

I do not remember, in talking with the President, that he ever agreed it was not the League itself that was at fault; that it had failed to work because the United States had stayed out, thus making it easier for England and France to use it to advance what they mistakenly believed to be their own interests.

What he did say frequently, however, before Pearl Harbor, was that if any good could come out of the Second World War it would be the opportunity afforded the Americans and the British to bring order out of the resulting chaos and, in particular, to disarm all those powers who in his belief had been the primary cause of so many of the wars of the preceding century. This thought was uppermost in his talks with Mr. Churchill at the Atlantic Charter meeting. And I feel sure it was what he had had in mind when he declared in an address at the very outset of the war in 1939, "It seems to me clear, even at the outbreak of this great war, that the influence of America should be consistent in seeking for humanity a final peace which will eliminate, as far as it is possible to do so, the continued use of force between nations."

I often felt during these years that in his attitude to the smaller countries outside the Western Hemisphere the President was unduly impatient. He maintained stubbornly that they should be satisfied if the English-speaking powers were able to assure them security from aggression, and in return should be willing to spend their national revenues upon education and upon raising living standards rather than upon armaments for which they would have no further need. He brushed aside all references to national pride, or to the age-old international hatreds of Eastern Europe. He dismissed as of little account the argument that no responsible government of a small country could be compelled to liquidate the military establishment upon which it believed the safety of the nation depended, unless the self-appointed policemen were prepared to occupy that country by force. He occasionally spoke of his project for an Anglo-American policing of the world as being "realistic." He would enumerate in considerable detail the various advantages that the peoples of the smaller countries would derive from such a policy of realism.

Another and altogether compelling motive for his failure to devote much thought to the details of international organization at that time was his preoccupation with his role as Commander-in-Chief of America's armed forces. He felt that until victory was clearly in sight his first obligation was to persuade the American people to subordinate every other consideration to winning the war. As I have already written,[3] "He was convinced that if he spoke to the American people, under the conditions which then existed, of post-war problems, they might be distracted from the cardinal objective of victory, and controversies might develop which would jeopardize national unity."

Finally, it must never be forgotten that the President's physical limitations gave the influence of those who saw him daily more than usual weight.

Many Democratic Congressional leaders were as outspoken as their Republican colleagues in asserting that no thought should be given to postwar problems; that they could be dealt with readily at a future peace conference; and that the attention of everyone in the Government and in the country should be dedicated exclusively to the war effort.

Mrs. Roosevelt as early as September 11, 1939, had publicly stated, "Let us pray that this time we will have the strength and foresight enough to plan a more permanent way of peace." But I know that her desire to see an international planning group set up was not shared by most of the President's White House advisers. Some of them, like Harry Hopkins, were instinctively inclined toward isolationism because of early environment and individual preference. Others, whose duties were largely confined to practical politics, strongly felt that anything resembling an appeal for American participation in

[3] Welles, Sumner, *Where Are We Heading?* (New York: Harper & Brothers, 1946), p. 18.

a postwar international organization would resurrect the old League of Nations controversy, and would be filled with political dynamite. They insisted that it was a dangerous, as well as an unnecessary, risk for the President to take.

These were all potent influences, and all the more potent because they coincided with certain of the President's own inclinations and prejudices. Yet the factors that brought about a complete change in his point of view proved in the long run to be more powerful still.

There were, first of all, the spectacular results of his own act in summoning the Inter-American Conference for the Maintenance of Peace that was held at Buenos Aires in 1936. During the five years that had since passed, the President had seen the rapid and steady growth of a regional organization composed of the twenty-one American republics. He had seen this organization unite the hemisphere against the Axis. Adolescent as it still was, and devoid as yet of any enforcement machinery, it had become a markedly successful example of international organization. His initiative, and its successful outcome, had met with unanimous acclaim in the United States.

He had also been profoundly impressed, and somewhat surprised, by the overwhelming enthusiastic reception that the American public had given the Atlantic Charter, The Charter represented a total break with the narrowly isolationist policies of the Harding, Coolidge, and Hoover Administrations. It declared that the United States, a nation still nominally neutral, would co-operate after the war with one of the major contestants in laying the foundations for a decent and peaceful world.

The long list of casualties within the family of nations for which the Nazis and Fascists had been responsible also affected his thinking. He had been revolted to the very depths of his soul in 1939 and 1940 by the prospect of the kind of world that Hitler, Mussolini and Stalin were so rapidly creating. His original reaction had been the concept of an Anglo-American policing job. But as time went on he saw that, appealing as the idea might be, it could not work. Britain, even though victorious, would be ruined at the end of the war. New and mighty revolutionary forces were arising throughout the world, and even the unparalleled power and resources of the United States could not cope with them alone. Some other answer had to be found.

But I am convinced that the determining factor was the immense impact of Pearl Harbor itself. The disaster brought home to him the full realization that today great power aggression can be forestalled only by effective collective security. In any event, the definitive change in Roosevelt's beliefs took place between the Atlantic Charter meeting and the spring of 1942.

The reason I feel that I can speak with authority on this point is that in the many talks I had with the President between 1936 and the summer of 1941 on the subject, he was never once willing to agree that an organization composed of all non-totalitarian countries was as yet feasible. Even less did he believe that the United States should or would attempt to participate in its construction. After Pearl Harbor, however, he became ever more steadily engrossed in the possibility of international organization. He made it plain that I might take it for granted that, when and if in his judgment the moment became ripe, he would assert American leadership in an attempt to create the kind of new world envisaged in the Atlantic Charter.

During the first part of 1942 it is quite true the President used frequently to say that he did not want to be drawn into the intensive studies of postwar settlements and world organization that were then already under way in the Department of State. This was primarily because he feared that if he did really get into them he would become so interested he might be tempted to devote less of his time and thought to the war effort itself. Also, I think, he wanted to keep an open mind regarding frontiers and other postwar problems, knowing that some compromises would be inevitable and that it would be unwise for him to become fixed in advance in his own convictions about the wisdom or justice of any particular solution.

Throughout that year, when I would tell him of the work being accomplished by the various committees in the Department of State, he would say, "What I expect you to do is to have prepared for me the necessary number of baskets and the necessary number of alternative solutions for each problem in the baskets, so that when the time comes all I have to do is to reach into a basket and fish out a number of solutions that I am sure are sound and from which I can make my own choice."

There are several accounts of the preliminary postwar research work begun in the State Department in 1942 by a small committee under my chairmanship. It was a new approach to a problem that the Department had previously handled in a wholly desultory fashion, and was authorized by the President exactly three weeks after Pearl Harbor.

There is nothing to be gained at this late date by relating the story of the endless bickering, and the internecine feuds that attended this essential undertaking. It is a depressing story at best, and it is a stale story now. Suffice it to say that during the first months of 1942 while I was Acting Secretary of State and, consequently, in actual charge of the work, the committee consisted of a few departmental officials, a handful of private citizens called in because of their special knowledge, and several Congressional leaders of both parties whom the President had authorized me to invite.[4]

Upon Secretary Hull's return in the late spring to Washington he at first refused to assume the chairmanship himself. When he finally did so later, I limited myself more and more to dealing with the purely technical aspects of international organization.

So many members were later added that the committee became unwieldy. Full committee meetings were generally sterile. Moreover, work to which the full time and energy of the subcommittees should have been exclusively devoted was periodically halted, sometimes for weeks, by the squabbles that so frequently broke out within the Department itself, and between the Department and other governmental agencies.

The most notorious of these was the row caused by a presidential order issued at the insistence of Henry Wallace, who was then Vice President, and who had been placed at the head of the newly created Board of Economic Warfare. The order gave the Board full authority to determine American postwar economic policy. It was obviously impossible for the State Department to plan intelligently or to recommend specific postwar settlements if it had no authority to decide what this

[4] Apart from the State Department officials named, the original committee was composed of the following members:

Senator Tom Connally
Senator Warren Austin
Mrs. Anne O'Hare McCormick
Myron C. Taylor
Hamilton Fish Armstrong
(Editor, *Foreign Affairs*)

Norman H. Davis
Dr. Isaiah Bowman (President, Johns Hopkins University)
Benjamin V. Cohen

country's economic policy was going to be. It was doubly impossible when this policy was to be determined by an agency that gave every indication of holding views diametrically opposed to those of the Secretary of State himself. An adjustment on paper was at length achieved. But it was an adjustment that never worked and, as long as the Board of Economic Warfare continued to function, conflicts with the Department of State were recurrent. They hampered inordinately the achievement of the major task that we had set for ourselves.

At the beginning of 1943, after I had been urging him to let me have the needed time, the President finally gave me an uninterrupted two hours at the White House, so that I might show him in written form the tentative conclusions so far reached by the Departmental Committee on International Organization. He saw me in his office late one afternoon after the day's appointments were ended, and after he had signed the basketfuls of urgent papers that flowed so endlessly across his desk. For once he was not in a digressive mood. He read very carefully the memoranda and charts that I placed before him.

At that stage the members of the departmental committee were almost unanimously of the opinion that any new world structure should be based on regional organizations similar to the Organization of American States. Each regional organization would periodically elect representatives to sit in a superior executive council to which supreme authority would be delegated by all the members of the United Nations. This executive council was to be composed of eleven members, seven to be elected by the regional organizations and the remaining four to be delegates of the United States, the Soviet Union, Great Britain, and

China. These four were to have permanent seats. While we recognized that each of the permanent members must have a veto right upon the use of any United Nations police force, the veto right proposed in this early draft was far more limited than that now granted the permanent members of the Security Council of the United Nations. What we suggested was that the use of military force could be ordered only if nine members of the supreme executive council voted affirmatively. But we felt that, if any one of the major powers was found guilty of aggression, it should not be permitted to veto the use of military sanctions imposed in its restraint.

As we look back over the events of the past five years, it is apparent that, had this limited veto right been agreed upon by the major powers at Dumbarton Oaks, and later by all the United Nations at San Francisco, most of the major obstacles that the United Nations has met would probably have been surmounted. But of course the Soviet Union would have refused to go into any international organization so constituted as to make possible collective action against Russian aggression. It was also very questionable whether the United States Senate would have ratified a Charter that did not leave the United States full latitude to determine at a given moment whether or not American military force should be employed.

This, in fact, was the main question that the President raised in my talk with him at that time. In general, he thought well of the project. However, he expressed considerable doubt whether regional organizations of the Near East and, for that matter, of Asia, could be expected to function efficiently in view of the lack of experience in self-government of most of the peoples in those areas.

The President held some exceedingly decided views about what nations should be given the ultimate authority to run the world during the first years after the war. There was naturally no question about the Soviet Union, Great Britain and the United States. But he was firm in his belief that France was not entitled at that juncture to be regarded as a major power. He felt that her recovery would be impossible if she continued to spend the greater part of her national revenues upon armaments and a standing army. Moreover, since Germany was to be dismembered, disarmed, and placed under international control, he saw no reason why France should continue to be a great military power. He was as strong in the view that Indo-China should promptly be granted independence as he was that Britain should restore Hongkong to China. He was equally determined that France should cede the port of Dakar to an international trusteeship, so that it might serve as a United Nations strategic base.

On the other hand, he was firmly resolved that China should from the outset be regarded as a major power, with a permanent seat on the supreme executive committee of the United Nations. He felt, he said, that recognition of China's status as one of the four major powers would prevent any charge that the white races were undertaking to dominate the world; that it would do much to stimulate Chinese patriotism and national pride and to pull together the various contending factions. A stable China, recognized as one of the great powers, would, he believed, be a barrier to Soviet ambitions in the Far East and serve also as a centripetal force of the utmost value in limiting the effects of the revolutionary upsurge in Asia.

I fully agreed with the President's conclusions concerning

China. But I believed that only harm would result if he persisted in his views about France. In fact, I argued with him for some time, pointing out that, if, as I hoped, Germany was to be disarmed and divided into a number of autonomous sovereign states, Great Britain alone could not be expected to balance in Western Europe the weight of the Soviet Union in Eastern Europe. It seemed to me that the loss of France as a strong, well-armed power, when there was no longer a strong and united Germany, would create a vacuum which the Soviet Union would inevitably be bound to fill. I doubt that my arguments had much effect at that time. Two years later, however, the President himself was to urge the Soviet Union to agree to let France participate in the military control of Germany. He also subsequently dropped all idea of French disarmament, probably as a result of the representations made to him by Mr. Churchill. Certainly I myself never heard him refer to it again. It may well be that the vigor with which he expressed these beliefs was due in no small part to his feeling that, if postwar France came under the domination of chauvinist leaders of the type of General de Gaulle, she would prove to be a major stumbling block to any healthy reorganization of the world.

The President had thoroughly digested the State Department's suggestions and had them very much in his mind when Anthony Eden, then British Secretary of State for Foreign Affairs, came to Washington in March, 1943, to canvass our Government's views on postwar problems. Shortly before his arrival, Mr. Churchill had delivered a speech in England which dealt with postwar problems. The Prime Minister had given the impression that he was interested solely in the creation of a regional European organization which the United States should be

invited to join, and that he had abandoned his earlier support
of a more general international organization. Mr. Eden made
it plain that he himself staunchly favored a new universal
organization, and deprecated the idea that the Prime Minister
really differed with him. This came out clearly at a meeting
with Mr. Eden which the President held in the White House
late in March and at which the British Ambassador, Secretary
Hull and myself were present.

The President outlined to the British Foreign Secretary the
kind of international organization that he had been thinking
over since my talk with him in January. He emphasized, rather
more strongly than I hoped he would, his belief that Great
Britain, the Soviet Union, and the United States, together
with China, must for a long time to come assert the right
to make all the basic decisions affecting the maintenance of
world order. As I remember the conversation—which was comprehensive, although at times it ran off on side issues—there
was already a very remarkable meeting of the minds between
the British and ourselves, even on the subject of trusteeships.
We were all in accord that the Russian stand on international
organization should be explored as rapidly as possible and that
the British and Americans should exchange views frequently until
the moment arrived when more formal conversations could take
place.

Again, at a dinner that I had at the British Embassy with
Mr. Eden and Lord Halifax before Mr. Eden returned to
London, we went over the entire field of international organization. Except for Mr. Eden's refusal even to consider the return
of Hongkong to China, there appeared to be no basic differences

whatever in the approach that the two English-speaking countries were making to postwar settlements.

In April the President invited me to go with him to Mexico where he was to make a long-deferred visit to President Avila Camacho. As I sat with him in the gathering twilight while the train passed through the low brown hills of northern Mexico on its way to Monterey, we talked over some of the more technical difficulties of having a United Nations built up on a foundation composed of regional organizations. I was especially struck, I well remember, by the President's reiteration of his belief that the great "question mark" was what Stalin would decide, and that it might well be that all our plans would prove to amount to no more than paper.

Upon my return to Washington a large part of my time was spent in hammering out with the members of the State Department committee a project that would eliminate some of the more obvious weaknesses in the earlier drafts.

In June of that year I gave the President the final blueprint of the United Nations as we had formulated it in the Department, and when I went to see him the day before he left for the Tehran Conference this draft with his own notes and suggested amendments was lying on his bed. The sketch drawn by the President at the Tehran meeting, reproduced in Sherwood's *Roosevelt and Hopkins,*[5] conveys simply but graphically the essential features of the project we had so often discussed.

In the meantime the major members of the United Nations, including China and so far excluding France, had issued at

[5] Sherwood, Robert, *Roosevelt and Hopkins* (New York: Harper & Brothers, 1948), p. 789.

Moscow a joint declaration announcing their intention to set up a universal organization. But it was at Tehran that Roosevelt and Stalin first discussed, around the table, the form which that organization should assume.

In view of Russian policy since the war, it is worth noting now that at Tehran Stalin not only opposed the inclusion of China as a major power—and China would never have been so accepted but for Roosevelt's ability to override 'the joint British and Russian objections—but that he also had come to favor the creation of regional councils to maintain peace, and the inclusion of the United States in such a regional council for Europe. Equally worthy of note is the President's blunt statement at the conference that the chief threat to the future peace of the world would be aggression by a major power. In that case, he said, it must automatically be subject to bombardment or invasion or both by the police force of the world organization.

No more definite agreement was reached at Tehran about the precise form the future world organization was to take. Yet unquestionably Roosevelt's personal conferences with Stalin dispelled misconceptions and misunderstandings on both sides, and helped materially to pave the way for the successful elaboration of what later became the United Nations Charter.

I agree with Robert Sherwood's estimate[6] that, "If there was any supreme peak in Roosevelt's career, I believe it might well be fixed at this moment, at the end of the Tehran conference."

Certainly there is every reason to think that the President returned from that meeting supremely optimistic, and confident that a decent world order could be set up after the victory with

[6] *Ibid.*, p. 799.

Russian as well as British co-operation assured. That he was satisfied with his own handiwork, these lines that he wrote me immediately after his return to Washington are proof[7]: "I want to tell you all about Cairo and Tehran. I think that as a roving Ambassador for the first time I did not 'pull any boners.'"

During the months between the Tehran conference and the four-power meeting at Dumbarton Oaks in Washington in the late summer of 1944, much was done to iron out the differences that had started to show themselves at Tehran. At Dumbarton Oaks the United States presented its "tentative proposals for a general international organization"; the British offered a separate draft; and the Soviet delegate set forth his Government's position.

As the President had indicated to me on our journey to Mexico, he had long since decided that differences such as these must be solved before the end of the war if the Soviet Union and the Western powers were ever to frame an international organization in which they could all take part. He had not missed the sinister significance of Stalin's insulting message to Churchill in the spring of 1944 threatening that, unless the Soviet Union could have its own way about Poland, Russian "co-operation in other spheres" would not be forthcoming. The President's own final correspondence with Stalin shows plainly how well he realized that the Kremlin's suspicions of the motives of the United States had by no means been dispelled. Nor was he blind to the signs that the Russian defeat of Hitler's armies had rapidly stimulated the Russian ego or to the fact that upon Germany's defeat the Soviet State would be by far the most powerful entity in Europe as well as in Asia.

[7] President Roosevelt to Sumner Welles, January 4, 1944.

He was for these very reasons more than ever convinced of the necessity of getting the Soviet Union to participate actively in the United Nations organization. With all the restrictions and limitations upon her course that this would provide, it was at this stage the best, and indeed the only, insurance against future trouble that could be devised. Yet, surprisingly, it was at this very juncture that the President succeeded so well in dealing with Stalin that there was little difficulty at Dumbarton Oaks in getting a joint agreement upon most of the principles that the United States regarded as basic.

The serious difficulties, in fact, were only two. One was whether the Soviet Union should be given what amounted to three votes in the Assembly instead of the one vote to which she was legitimately entitled. The other, in reality far more important, was whether the right of veto granted the permanent members on the Security Council should be unlimited, or whether, as the British and the Americans desired, the veto should be restricted to proposals for the use of sanctions in disputes in which the major powers were not themselves participants.

The Soviet Union was adamant in her insistence that every great power should have the right not only to veto the imposition of sanctions by the Security Council against itself, but also to veto the mere consideration by the Security Council of any international dispute in which that power might claim it was a participant. The Soviet Government at first threatened that it would never join an international organization which did not guarantee it an unlimited veto power. Yet here again the President by direct negotiations with Moscow—undertaken, it may be remembered, during an exhausting Presidential campaign—

secured agreement on a compromise formula which was later officially approved at the Yalta Conference.

This compromise admitted the Soviet contention that the veto might legitimately be employed by a major power to prevent sanctions against itself. But the Soviet Union conceded the American contention that the veto should not include the right to prevent the Security Council's consideration of any dispute, even if a major power was a participant in it. The compromise formula, therefore, made it possible for the Security Council to ventilate publicly all future controversies in which Russia or any other great power might be involved.

The criticism of the President for this compromise formula, which was made public after the Yalta Conference, has been widespread. From our own standpoint the formula is, of course, imperfect, since it admits the right of the Soviet Union to prevent the Security Council from imposing sanctions upon her, if she commits an act of aggression. Collective action to check the aggression must, therefore, be taken in other ways. Yet as we saw when Russia threatened Iran in 1946, the airing of such disputes by the Security Council, with the consequent impact on world opinion, can be extremely effective. And in the case of attack on South Korea in 1950, fifty-three members of the United Nations were able to join in armed resistance to the aggression, despite the Soviet Union's use of every form of blackmail, intimidation, and parliamentary filibuster.

Can any objective observer who believes in a universal international organization as the only efficient means of securing peace seriously maintain that in the light of conditions as they existed in 1945 was it not far better to obtain a United Nations of which Russia would be a member from the outset—particularly when the Charter itself was to be open to amendment—than to risk having no United Nations at all by refusing to compromise?

The President's concession that the Soviet republics of the Ukraine and Byelo-Russia be invited to become members of the Assembly, whereby the Soviet Union secured three votes in that body, was one that he made reluctantly. At the outset he was determined to refuse. He felt that he could convince Stalin that it would be wiser not to press his demand by telling him that he would agree provided Stalin also agreed that the United States should be given forty-eight votes in the General Assembly, one for each of the sovereign states in the American Union. The President finally gave in, I can only assume, because of his belief that the question was not in itself of practical importance —as, in fact, it was not—and because the British strongly felt that the concession might keep the Soviet from opposing the voting rights of the members of the British Commonwealth—as, in fact, it did. Finally, I believe he conceded the point because he recognized that the Soviet Union was joining an organization in which they could count upon only a small handful of thick and thin adherents, and that the addition of two more sure votes for Moscow in the Assembly would be psychologically wise without at the same time endangering the needed numerical supremacy of the free nations.

There were few among his advisers in 1945 who were not in wholehearted agreement with him, and who did not share his belief that the nations bound together in the common struggle against Germany and Japan should likewise bind themselves together through the United Nations organization in a similar effort to procure a peaceful world after the fighting was done.

Of those who disagreed, Henry L. Stimson was perhaps the foremost. In a memorandum which he wrote on January 23, 1945, Mr. Stimson made these observations.[8]

The job of the four big nations is presently to establish a guaranty of peace in the atmosphere of which the world organization can be set going.

This will necessarily include the settlement of all territorial acquisitions in the shape of defense posts which each of these four powers may deem to be necessary for their own safety in carrying out such a guaranty of world peace.

For substantially this purpose, at the end of the last war President Wilson proposed a Joint Covenant of Guaranty by Britain and America of the security of France as the pillar of Western Europe. But the mistake was made of not securing that guaranty before the second step of creating the League of Nations whose safety was in large part to be dependent upon such a guaranty. As a result the League of Nations lacked a foundation of security which ultimately proved fatal to it.

I think we are in danger of making a similar mistake by attempting to formulate the Dumbarton organization before we have discussed and ironed out the realities which may exist to enable the four powers to carry out their mission. . . .

Any attempt to finally organize a Dumbarton organization will necessarily take place in an atmosphere of unreality until these preliminary foundations are established. The attitude of numerous minor nations who have no real responsibility, but plenty of vocal power and logical arguments, will necessarily be different from that of the large powers who have to furnish the real security. . . .

For all these reasons I think we should not put the cart before the horse. We should by thorough discussion between the three or four great powers endeavor to settle, so far as we can, an accord upon the general area of these fundamental problems. We should endeavor to

[8] Stimson, Henry L., *On Active Service in Peace and War* (New York: Harper & Brothers, 1948), p. 603.

secure a covenant of guaranty of peace or at least an understanding of the conditions upon which such a general undertaking of mutual guaranty could be based.

Mr. Stimson's memorandum was addressed to the Secretary of State. I do not know whether or not the President himself read it. Given the condition of his health, which was then already failing rapidly, and given the desire of the White House secretariat at this time to relieve him of the necessity of reading departmental memoranda, I doubt whether he ever studied the document.

With very real admiration for Secretary Stimson's qualities as one of the most enlightened statesmen of modern times, I still believe that the President was altogether right and that Mr. Stimson was altogether wrong.

Had the four powers, after the defeat of Germany and of Japan, undertaken, as Mr. Stimson suggested, to reach a common agreement upon the "settlement of territorial acquisitions in the shape of defense posts" which each thought it might need, what would Russia's demands have been in Asia, in the Near East, and in Europe? We now know, at least to some extent, what Russia's ambitions really are. Would there have been any likelihood that the British or ourselves would have been willing to concede Russian so-called "defense posts" in Turkey, in Iran, in the Adriatic, or in the Mediterranean? Would we have been willing to agree that the Soviet Union was to become the overlord not only of China but of the rest of Southeast Asia? That was precisely what we had done our utmost to prevent Japan from becoming.

Mr. Stimson's proposals, it seems to me, might have had considerable cogency if the four police powers had consisted of four democratic and Western nations. Had his proposals been adopted, however, with the Soviet Union as one of the four great police powers, the result in 1945 would have been an experiment in sheer power politics in which neither morals nor principles would have had any play, and in which Russia would have held all the trump cards.

Actually, what Stimson proposed, though needless to say from wholly different motives, was precisely what Stalin himself had originally had in mind. The Stimson proposal in reality implied, not the establishment of a world organization founded upon justice and international law, but an alliance of great military powers which would assume the right to carve up the world into four zones of great power influence. How long would it have been before the most powerful of them would have sought to assert that right without interference from its partners?

Roosevelt's decision that the postwar period should begin with a working universal international organization in which the Soviet Union would be an active participant, and in which all the lesser nations would have an equal right to make their grievances heard, to secure redress and jointly to search for peace, seems to me to have offered the American people a far better assurance for the future.

I have known no man in American public life who believed more implicitly than President Roosevelt that the hope of the world lay in the renewal of peoples' faith in democracy. He saw more clearly than most of his contemporaries that the power and the menace of communism came from the fanatical faith of its prophets and of its addicts, even more than from the military force and vast potential resources of the Soviet Union. To him communism was a bloody, stifling and intolerable ideology.

Yet he frankly recognized the appeal that its promise of economic security held for millions of starving and downtrodden men and women in many parts of the world. But he believed communism would never prevail provided democracy became a living reality here in the United States and in the other free nations, and provided those who cherished democracy would strive for its supremacy with the same self-sacrificing fervor shown by the Marxists in fighting for their creed.

Beyond and above all else, he had reached the conclusion that communism's stoutest ally was war, and that only in a world at peace could the basic tenets of democracy ultimately triumph.

He was one of that rare and select number who "see visions and dream dreams."

Remember the phrases in his final undelivered speech, the one on which he was working when he died:

The work, my friends, is peace, more than an end of this war— an end to the beginnings of all wars, yes, an end, forever, to this impractical, unrealistic settlement of the differences between governments by the mass killings of people.

It was to that work that Franklin Roosevelt devoted all his waning strength in the closing months of his life.

CHAPTER VIII

Policy for Today

ANTHONY EDEN came back to Washington for a brief visit in the autumn of 1950. Talking with him at that time about some of the problems of the past and of the present, I asked him if he didn't feel, looking back over the events of the past five years, that the policy which the Soviet Government had pursued up to the end of June, 1945, had undergone a radical transformation after the Potsdam conference. Mr. Eden said that he agreed. He then told me this story of his first visit to Moscow after Pearl Harbor.

Shortly before Mr. Churchill came to Washington at the end of December, 1941, to initiate his long series of wartime conferences with President Roosevelt, he had sent Mr. Eden, who was then Foreign Secretary, to Moscow to try to find, through direct negotiations with Stalin, a basis for satisfactory understanding between the British and Soviet governments. Mr. Eden said that one of his talks with Stalin took place late at night in Stalin's apartment in the Kremlin. At that very moment the Germans were battering at Moscow's gates. It was perhaps the most critical hour in the Red Army's resistance to the Nazi onslaught. In the midst of the conversation Stalin suddenly interjected the observation that Hitler had proved himself to be a man of extraordinary genius. He had succeeded in building up a ruined and divided people into a mighty world power within an incredibly short space of time; he had succeeded in so regimenting the Germans that all elements were completely subservient to his will. "But," Stalin added, "Hitler has shown he has one fatal defect. He does not know where to stop."

Mr. Eden said that at that juncture he couldn't help smiling. Stalin, who was intensely serious, at first seemed irritated, and demanded to know the reason for his amusement. But then before Mr. Eden could reply, Stalin answered his own question: "I realize now why you are smiling, Mr. Eden. You are wondering if I myself will know where to stop. But I can assure you that I will always know where to stop."

Up to the time of the Potsdam conference in August, 1945, there seemed every reason to believe that Stalin would fulfill the promise he had given Mr. Eden four years before. Except in the case of Poland, where there were signs that a controversy between the Soviet Union and the Western powers might be looming, there had been no serious dispute between the Kremlin and the governments of the United States and of Great Britain. A compromise agreement had been reached on the Charter of the United Nations. Authoritative spokesmen for the American and British governments have publicly attested that up to mid-summer of 1945 the Soviet Government had faithfully carried out all its military commitments to its major allies, and had given reasonable evidence of sincerely desiring to co-operate through the United Nations in the creation of a world in which there need be no clash between democracy and Soviet communism. But since then it has daily become more plain that the Kremlin has failed to recognize the application to its own course of Stalin's analysis of Hitler. The great question today is whether the

Western nations can, before it is too late, make the rulers of
the Russian people prove that they do know where to stop.

And that question necessarily raises a series of other questions.

Is this total change in Russian policy and Russian tactics due
primarily to internal causes such as the increasing influence of
the Red Army on Soviet policy? Is it due to the fact that with
Stalin's rise to unprecedented power his agents abroad have
been afraid to tell him the truth about conditions in the West?
Is it due perhaps to the fact that when Stalin and his advisers
had their first chance to appraise the new leaders of the West
at Potsdam they came to the conclusion that a course of all-out
aggressive expansion had become as feasible as it was tempting?
Or is this reversal of the Soviet Union's earlier policy due primarily to the errors in policy and strategy of which the Western
Powers, and in particular the United States, have been guilty
since the close of the war.

Since the days of the Bolshevik revolution a basic theory of
the Soviet state has always been that in time communism was
bound to spread all over the world. But it had seemed during
the years of the American-British-Soviet alliance, and especially
after Stalin's abolition of the Comintern, that the Russian dictatorship had decided to abandon force and subversion as the
most effective means of hastening world revolution, and to await
the postwar economic collapse it anticipated, which it was confident would quite as surely bring about the final downfall
of Western capitalism. As I have previously indicated, domestic
developments in all probability played their part in causing
the Politburo to revise its tactics. Yet if our own mistakes also
helped to make this change possible, it will not be a wholly

useless effort to speculate upon what the course of events might have been had this Government adopted different measures and made different decisions at certain determining moments during the past five years.

It may perhaps seem presumptuous to try to imagine what Franklin Roosevelt would have done had he lived out his final term as President. Yet in a few cases I am also going to make this attempt. Since I was privileged to work closely with him during the better part of ten years, I believe I have some knowledge of his basic intentions and of the convictions which guided him in his handling of our foreign relations.

If we ourselves are in any way responsible for the change in Soviet policy that became evident after the Potsdam conference, where did we make our first mistakes? What have been our subsequent errors of omission and of commission?

Surely the first, and in its consequences one of the gravest, of these mistakes was our withdrawal in May, 1945, of the American forces that had liberated Czechoslovakia, and our failure to insure unimpeded access to Berlin from the West. The plan for the purely military occupation of Germany and of Austria by the allies had been, it is true, agreed upon in principle at Yalta. But the plan was in sufficiently general terms to have made it wholly possible for the positions of the American, Russian, and British armies at the time of Germany's surrender to have remained in *status quo* until the Chiefs of Government had reached a firm agreement upon the future administration of Germany, and upon the details of the plans by which the liberated countries were to have their sovereign independence restored.

It is now an open secret that Prime Minister Churchill

repeatedly requested President Truman to agree to keep the American forces in Czechoslovakia and to keep the gates of Berlin open to the West until a meeting between the President, Stalin, and himself had taken place, and that his pleas met with an adamant refusal. President Truman's refusal was presumably dictated by his desire not to take any action that could arouse Moscow's suspicion of our objectives. On the other hand, the maneuvers of the Russian armies in Austria as well as in Germany had already caused us justifiable concern. There can today be little question that, had we maintained these positions, the American and British representatives would have arrived at Potsdam with a far greater bargaining power, and with far more prospect of securing postwar settlements in Central and Eastern Europe that would assure those people their ultimate freedom.

It is an equally open secret that Mr. Churchill is convinced that, had Franklin Roosevelt still been President at the time his requests were made, the American Government would have acted in compliance with them.

We knew that after every war in which Russia's armies had been victorious the influence of her military leaders had become a potent factor, and had been exercised in behalf of imperialist expansion. It would have seemed a reasonable measure of insurance at that moment for the representatives of the Western powers to see to it that the Soviet Union should not accumulate overwhelming force throughout the whole of Eastern Europe and that a restraining Western military pressure should continue until the essential political accords had been concluded.

However, since Mr. Churchill's requests were refused, the East-West line had already been drawn when the Potsdam conference took place. Except for Trieste and Greece, the Russian armies were in physical control of all the territory east of the Stettin-Trieste Line. From that time on all the Western allies could do to procure the execution in spirit as well as in letter of the Yalta agreements relating to the establishment of "free and democratic" governments in the Eastern European countries was necessarily limited to the dispatch of mere appeals and remonstrances.

The influence of the Western powers upon a totalitarian government that "only respects force" was rapidly diminished after the defeat of Japan by the headlong demobilization of the American armies overseas. Yet at Potsdam an American President representing what was then the mightiest power on earth could still have secured from Stalin an agreement upon the major provisions of the peace treaties ultimately to be negotiated with a new German Government. At Tehran and at Yalta Stalin had specifically expressed his conformity with President Roosevelt's long-held view that Germany should be decentralized in such a manner as to enable the ancient German states, that had for so many centuries before 1870 enjoyed their sovereign autonomy, to regain their independence should they so desire, and that in no event should the Germany of the future include Prussia. So far as I can ascertain, little, if any, consideration was given at Potsdam to this prior agreement. I am confident that if President Roosevelt had survived the implementation of that decision would have had first place on his agenda.

Yet it should have been a foregone conclusion in the minds of President Truman's advisers that every week that passed after the victory was won would make it increasingly difficult for the demobilizing Western powers to reach an agreement with a mobilized Soviet Union upon a German occupation policy and peace treaty that would prove satisfactory from our point of view. And surely it must have been equally clear that any future developments that made possible either the resurgence of a militaristic Pan-German Reich or the amalgamation of German technical skill and industrial capacity with Communist-dominated manpower and natural resources, would inevitably end all of mankind's hopes for a peaceful Europe or a peaceful world.

It should have been equally apparent to them, if they had any familiarity with the history of Europe since 1917, or any knowledge of the bases of Soviet policy since the Communist revolution of that year, that to the Russians Germany is the core of the European problem. The Communist leaders have been consistently and fanatically convinced that if the Soviet Union can get the German people on her side she can control the whole of Europe. They have never wavered in their devotion to that end.

Nothing, consequently, could have been more tragically shortsighted than for the spokesmen for the United States and Great Britain to leave Potsdam without getting from the Soviet Government an accord that would give the West satisfactory assurance that Germany could not be drawn into the Soviet orbit.

At the Potsdam conference Mr. Churchill and Mr. Eden were replaced after a few days, as a result of the British national elections, by Mr. Attlee and Mr. Bevin. Both Mr. Attlee and Mr. Bevin had been members of Mr. Churchill's War Cabinet. They had as advisers officials and civil servants thoroughly qualified to offer expert counsel. President Truman had such an advantage only in the military sphere. Except for Admiral Leahy, none of his close advisers, and least of all his new Secretary of State, James F. Byrnes, possessed either knowledge, understanding, or experience in foreign relations. While there were on hand two or three able representatives of the State Department, they were all specialists who had no broad knowledge of the larger European or world scene.

At the time of the Potsdam conference the United States was at the peak of her political and military power. Yet largely because of the lack of preparedness, lack of knowledge, and lack of vision of her representatives at that conference, Potsdam marked the beginning of the rapid deterioration in American political and military influence that has continued unchecked until this year of 1951. We were faced at Potsdam with a tough partner thoroughly versed and skilled in the game of power politics. We were outplayed in every move. As a result, when the conference adjourned Germany and Austria were left in a state of confusion worse confounded, with the Eastern and Western occupying powers already pursuing wholly divergent policies. Far worse, there was no prospect of achieving unity of purpose or of policy, and no prospect of any four-power agreement upon a German peace treaty that might bring security to the world.

The only constructive step as far as Europe was concerned appeared to be the agreement to create a Council of Foreign Ministers which was to be entrusted with solving all the problems that the conference had left unsolved.

When this newly formed Council held its first meeting in London a few weeks later, the United States showed herself to be as wholly unprepared to cope with the basic issues underlying the reconstruction of Europe as she had been at Potsdam. Secretary of State Byrnes represented this country. His intentions were doubtless of the best. But he had no perception of the fundamental issues that were at stake. He also was unable to realize the importance of the old maxim that no power can exercise influence through its diplomacy unless its foreign policy is known to be dependable. As merely one evidence of this deficiency in him, Mr. Byrnes on his way to London declared that the United States favored a certain solution for the disposition of Italy's colonies; but upon his arrival there he announced that we favored a totally different solution.

This first session of the Council of Foreign Ministers did nothing except accentuate the radical differences between the Soviet Union and the Western powers that had become apparent at Potsdam, and lessen the confidence of the Western European peoples in the ability of the United States to exercise effective leadership in world affairs. There can be no question that the rapid growth of the Communist popular strength through Western Europe during the autumn and winter of 1945-1946 was due largely to this growing lack of faith in the United States and to the belief of distressed and confused peoples that the Soviet Union would be the best bet after all.

Perhaps the most far-reaching of the errors perpetrated by this Government during those fateful autumn months of 1945 was the "mission to Moscow" which Secretary of States Byrnes felt impelled to undertake toward the close of the year.

Here was a man who during his years of service in the United States Senate had never even been a member of the Foreign Relations Committee; a man whose brief service in the United States Supreme Court and as a presidential assistant had never

brought him into touch with foreign affairs, and whose knowledge of our foreign relations during the war period was limited
to what he might have learned as an observer at the Yalta conference. Here was a man whose ignorance of even the rudi-
mentary facts of international life was so profound that it was the
subject for amazed comment among a number of Washington
correspondents when at one press conference he was unable to
list the countries bordering upon the Black Sea. Yet, inspired by
the conviction that he was truly serving the cause of world peace,
this was the man who took it upon himself to make agreements
with Stalin that were to no small extent responsible for the rapid
consolidation of Russia's control over Eastern Europe and for
the equally rapid growth of Russian prestige in the rest of Europe.

The most fatal of the decisions that Mr. Byrnes reached at
Moscow made a mockery of the fundamental principles of the
Yalta agreements covering the liberated countries of Europe, and
gave the Soviet Government the opportunity to get an immediate
stranglehold over all the nations east of the Stettin-Trieste line.

At Yalta Roosevelt, Churchill and Stalin had signed an agreement which proclaimed "the right of all peoples to choose the
form of Government under which they will live" and "the restoration of sovereign rights and self-government to those peoples
who have been forcibly deprived of them by the aggressor
nations." And in this same agreement they had declared that

. . . to foster the conditions in which the liberated people may
exercise these rights, the three Governments will *jointly* assist the
people in any liberated European state . . . to form interim governmental authorities broadly representative of all democratic elements
in the population and pledged to the earliest possible establishment

through free elections of governments responsive to the will of the people; and to facilitate where necessary the holding of such elections.

It was this pledge, which Roosevelt and Churchill had brought Stalin to agree to, and upon whose realization democracy and individual freedom in Eastern Europe clearly depended, that with an unparalleled levity Mr. Byrnes now discarded.

Evidently he was under the impression that he could negotiate with the Russian dictator the same kind of political deal that he had been accustomed to engineer in the cloakroom of the United States Senate. In any case, apparently not realizing the significance of what he was conceding, Mr. Byrnes agreed that this Yalta pledge might be construed to provide for the merely nominal participation of two opposition representatives in the interim governments of the Eastern European countries that Russia had occupied—and in which Communist agents selected by Mr. Vishinsky were already the dominating factors. It is obvious that such governments could not by the wildest stretch of the imagination be regarded as "broadly representative of all democratic elements." Necessarily it was only a matter of a short time before the two representatives of the opposition parties were eliminated. And necessarily, under governments controlled by a ruthless Communist machine, the very idea of free elections became farcical and one-party tickets became the rule. The ability of the United States and of Great Britain to act "jointly" with the Soviet Union in assisting the "liberated" peoples of Eastern Europe to establish "through free elections governments responsive to the will of the people" was thus ended.

Nothing could have done more to destroy the faith of the peoples of Eastern Europe and, for that matter, of Central

Europe, in the desire and capacity of the United States to help them toward real liberation; nothing could have done more to pave the way for that tragic obliteration of all vestiges of democracy in Czechoslovakia which was to come two years later. From that time on there could be no more hope that the United States could prevent or even retard the construction of the Iron Curtain.

As we look back over this depressing record, there are nevertheless to be found two outstandingly constructive moves—one of them American and one of them French in origin. Both helped measurably to lessen Soviet influence in Central and Western Europe, and both were designed to promote European rehabilitation and to lessen postwar tensions.

The first of these, of course, is the Marshall Plan.

No one who has visited Western Europe recurrently during the years since the end of the war can have failed to see how magnificently successful this effort of ours to help other free and democratic peoples help themselves has proved to be. Living standards have steadily been raised, rehabilitation and reconstruction have gone on at a rapid pace, the psychology of millions of despairing and hopeless people has been transformed. By making it possible for the men and women of the devastated, war-torn countries of Europe to achieve, or at least to foresee, economic security, the Marshall Plan has greatly lessened the extent of the insidious appeal of Soviet communism. Under the wise and able administration of Paul Hoffman and of his assistants, ECA has outstandingly aided the democratic cause and the containment of Soviet expansion. Here and there, undoubtedly, particularly at the beginning of the program, mistakes in policy were made and administration was sometimes inefficient, but in the over-all estimate an unprejudiced observer cannot question that the billions spent by the American taxpayers in carrying out the Marshall Plan program have been more than balanced by what has been gained in the way of security for the United States.

When I was in Western Europe in the summer of 1950 I had the opportunity of talking with many of the members of Western European governments as well as with leaders of the opposition parties, most of whom had been friends of mine for many years. Not one of them failed to recognize the outstanding contribution that the United States had made through the Marshall Plan toward rebuilding a free and democratic world. A great majority of them admitted that without it there would have been little chance of preventing the establishment of Communist governments in such countries as Italy and France.

Yet even before the Korean debacle two overshadowing anxieties oppressed the hearts and minds of the Western European peoples from Norway all the way to Greece. One was the fear that a new world war might break out and that their own countries once more would become a battleground. The other overshadowing worry was whether the English-speaking peoples would once more, as they did after the First World War, permit the rearmament of Germany before adequate safeguards made it impossible for the new Germany again to make war upon her neighbors, either with or without the backing of the Soviet Union.

It is for this reason that the second great constructive move regarding Western Europe possessed such supreme importance. This was the proposal of the French Government known as the Schuman Plan, providing for the international control of all the coal, iron and steel production of Western Europe, including that of Germany. It constituted the one practical method by which Germany's war potential could be surrounded with adequate safeguards. It is the only plan so far proposed that could remove from the hearts of the French people their wholly legitimate and understandable fear of future attack if Germany is now rearmed. It is the surest way to bring the German people back as law-abiding and peaceful members of the family of nations. I cannot conceive of a greater incentive toward the creation of a federated and united Europe, in which the German people can eventually play a constructive and worthy part.

After the Schuman Plan had been announced the American Government gave it its emphatic endorsement. The British Labor Government, however, opposed it for what were apparently purely ideological reasons. The great industrial interests of England were equally strong in their opposition because the project would limit their freedom of action. While the continental countries have made such progress as they could in the face of British opposition, the Schuman Plan can never become really viable unless the British co-operate. And unless the industrial and mineral resources of the Ruhr are placed under rigid international control there is no Frenchman, and for that matter no Belgian and no Dutchman, who will not believe that German rearmament direly menaces his own safety.

By the early winter of 1949 the menacing aspects of Soviet policy had made the Atlantic Defense Pact a practical necessity. Yet who could have imagined a few short years ago that the English-speaking peoples, pledged to impose permanent disarmament upon a defeated Germany, would now, in spite of all French remonstrances, be pressing a reluctant Western Germany to create immediately fifteen to twenty divisions? This upon the pretext that German manpower is r‸ ‚uired if the Atlantic Pact is to be successful.

The issue here presented seems to me to be even graver in its implications than the issues that have recently arisen in this country's relations with the Far East.

Had a new crisis in Soviet-American relations not occurred and had the Schuman Plan as it was originally conceived been now operating, the French, with their acute and logical comprehension of European affairs, would have been satisfied in the winter of 1951 that their security was safeguarded, that a new and better relationship between the French and German peoples was at last possible and that, consequently, German participation on equal terms in the defense of Western Europe was admissible. The fact is, however, that the Schuman Plan remains on paper, and many of France's most farsighted statesmen are convinced that without such a safeguard a rearmed Western Germany will become the ally, rather than the opponent, of the Soviet Union. Nothing, therefore, could be better calculated to inflame French sentiment against the English-speaking peoples and to increase the popular strength of the French Communist Party than the Anglo-American plan for German rearmament.

Nor is there any evidence that the people of Western Germany or their leaders, whether Conservative or Socialist, have any desire to adopt the rearmament projects that are being urged upon them, except as a means of procuring new concessions from the occupying powers. They are fully aware that at the best considerable time must elapse before German rearmament could become effective, and that, were Western Germany to resist a Soviet attack upon Western Europe, they themselves would be in the front lines.

Finally, if we are to be realistic, given the acute tension now existing in our relations with the Soviet Union, how can we fail to admit that any Russian Government, even a government far more pacific and conciliatory, must inevitably regard as a threat to Russian security our rearmament of the country that in 1917 forced them to accept the shameful peace of Brest-Litovsk, and in 1941 invaded and ravaged their homeland?

How can we regard the minor military assistance, which is all that the Western powers can presently hope to gain by German rearmament, as outweighing the immense future dangers which such a step involves? It seems at times that the English-speaking peoples, and particularly the American people, are incapable of learning by experience, however tragic and however recent that experience may be.

We are told that the Germans of Western Europe are today war-weary and disheartened. During the years of the Weimar Republic both Great Britain and the United States also believed the German people to be war-weary and disheartened. Over the same French opposition that we see today, Great Britain then not only permitted, but actually connived at, German rearmament. We Americans poured hundreds of millions of dollars into Germany in the form of loans. It was those policies which were directly responsible for the Second World War.

After 1933 both the British and ourselves soon discovered that the German people whom we had thought disheartened and war-weary had very quickly indeed become a great, regimented military force bent once more upon a course of aggression and of world domination. German rearmament today, before the German people have shown any change of heart, before any adequate safeguards have been set up to control Germany's capacity to make war, and at the precise moment when a rearmed Germany may well become an asset, rather than an obstacle, to Soviet expansion, seems to me, I must confess, an exact repetition of the fatal blunder which England and America committed a scant thirty years ago.

I am well aware that the opinions I have expressed run counter to those of many of the ablest of my fellow citizens as well as to those of such a great Englishman as Winston Churchill. To that, I can only submit that it was largely these same men who in the 1920's believed that in rearming Germany we would be erecting a barrier to the spread of Soviet Communism. The fatal outcome of that policy we have all witnessed. What has happened since to give us any assurance that similar results will not follow if we repeat the experiment? Franklin Roosevelt often declared that, whatever the nature of the peace, it must at least provide for German disarmament until such time as the German people had offered a practical demonstration of their spiritual regeneration. Remembering this, I cannot for one moment imagine that he would now join his wartime colleague, Winston Churchill, in supporting any policy that calls for German rearmament.

Like other human beings, men in high authority, no matter how towering their stature, no matter how vast their knowledge, or how great their genius, possess their peculiar weaknesses and defects. And these Franklin Roosevelt would have been the first to admit that he by no means lacked.

To me, as I suppose to all others who worked closely with him in the field of foreign policy, one of his most exasperating idiosyncrasies was his almost invariable unwillingness to dictate any memoranda of his conversations with foreign statesmen or foreign diplomatic representatives in Washington as a record to inform and guide those who were running the Department of State. But a peculiarity that was far more serious in its result was his deep-rooted prejudice against the members of the American Foreign Service and against the permanent officials of the Department of State. He was quite willing to appoint qualified and experienced Foreign Service officers as Ambassadors and Ministers abroad. In fact no President, before or since, has appointed so large a percentage of his diplomatic representatives in foreign countries from the American Foreign Service. But it was very rare indeed that President Roosevelt could be persuaded to bring into White House conferences on foreign policy any of those State Department specialists who had devoted a lifetime to the study of some particular country or region, and who could have given him the detailed information and authoritative viewpoint that he very frequently lacked.

At the Cairo conferences with the Generalissimo and Madame Chiang Kai-shek, the President had at his side no expert adviser on Far Eastern affairs. At Yalta also such advice was lacking. If the President had had with him at those two conferences so authoritative and keen-minded an expert on Far Eastern affairs, for example, as Dr. Stanley Hornbeck, who had for many years been the State Department's Political Adviser on the Far East, a number of defects in the Cairo and Yalta agreements on Asia might well have been avoided.

Nevertheless, the main lines of the policies laid down in those agreements will, in my judgment, be proved with the passage of time to have been sound in the light of conditions at the time they were concluded. I have tried to show in previous chapters that it is because the present Administration departed from those policies that the United States and the United Nations now face a crisis in the Far East.

Had President Roosevelt survived, I think it is probably true that, like his successor, he would have made every effort to bring about a peaceful adjustment of the increasingly violent altercations between Chiang Kai-shek's Government and the Chinese Communists, just as during the war he tried to prevent the two Chinese factions from fighting each other rather than the Japanese. But I am equally confident that, considering Moscow's tactics in imposing Communist governments on Poland and other Eastern European countries in the autumn of 1945 and 1946, he would never have permitted his representative in China to pave the way for a repetition of the same tactics in the Far East by trying to browbeat Chiang Kai-shek, as General Marshall did, into bringing representatives of the Chinese Communist Party into the Chinese Cabinet. It is, in fact, a strange anomaly that this Government in 1946 urged Prime Minister de Gasperi of Italy to oust the Communists who were then in the Italian Cabinet. De Gasperi's decision to take that step was in the highest degree salutary. It was probably the chief reason why a successful Communist *coup d'état* in Italy that year was prevented. Yet in the autumn of that same year General Marshall, as President Truman's special representative in China, was informing Chiang Kai-shek that all American assistance would be withdrawn unless he "broadened" his government by appointing Communists as well as other "liberal" elements to the Cabinet.

The spokesmen for the more liberal elements in this country who have supported the present Administration's policy in the Far East insist that the corruption, inefficiency, oppression, and cruelty of the Kuomintang regime made it impossible for the

United States to continue to support that regime if she was to retain the friendship of the Chinese people. Impartial observers of developments in China since the defeat of Japan will readily confirm most of the charges that these critics bring against the Chinese Nationalist Government. Yet, if we were to pursue our own national interests realistically, what was the alternative to backing the Nationalist Government?

During the years before 1939 I was repeatedly amazed that only a handful of the higher officials in Washington had ever read Hitler's *Mein Kampf*, although in that book, for all who cared to see, were set forth in the fullest detail all Hitler's beliefs and all his intentions. It would be interesting to know how many of those chiefly responsible for our Far Eastern policy since 1945 are familiar with the writings of Lenin or with the cardinal doctrines that he and Stalin laid down with regard to the Far East. For these show that one of the basic tenets of Soviet Communism has always been that once the billion and a half men and women in China, India and Southeast Asia have been indoctrinated with communism, and are linked to the people of Russia in the struggle to bring about the world triumph of the Communist ideology, the immense superiority in manpower of that alliance will insure the defeat of Western capitalism. Certainly American policy in the Far East between 1945 and 1950 has expedited rather than retarded the achievement of that aim.

I was privileged to know well and to work closely for some years with Dr. Hu-Shih, who was Chinese Ambassador in Washington at the time this country entered the war. I have never known a more devoted patriot or a man who more ardently desired that his country become a true democracy. No loyal Chinese could have clarified the gist of the whole problem in more succinct and moving terms than did Dr. Hu-Shih in an appeal which he made to this Government in December, 1948. The American Ambassador in China reported him as having then said,

Communism is so implacable and intolerant, so diabolically thorough in its indoctrination, and so ruthless in enforcing its totalitarian control even in China that Chiang Kai-shek should be supported despite his shortcomings, because he alone sees this and has been uncompromising in resisting it.

Because that appeal was disregarded we have not only failed to gain that friendship of the Chinese people which the Administration and its "liberal" supporters believed could be gained by withdrawing American support from Chiang, but we face the probability that before long those traditionally friendly people will be poisoned by vicious and effective Communist propaganda with a fanatical hatred for the American people.

We might profitably recall here the story that Jonathan Daniels tells in his book *The Man of Independence*.[1] He relates a conversation that he had with Admiral William D. Leahy, who was one of President Roosevelt's closest advisers and who later served in the same capacity with President Truman.

"I was present when Marshall was going to China," Admiral Leahy told me. "He said he was going to tell Chiang that he had to get on with the Communists or without help from us. He said the same thing when he got back. I thought he was wrong then, both times."

Events have shown conclusively that Admiral Leahy was right both times.

As I have already emphasized, this Government's record in Korea between 1945 and June, 1950, has been a record of ineffi-

[1] Daniels, Jonathan, *The Man of Independence* (Philadelphia: J. B. Lippincott, 1950), p. 317.

ciency and of vacillation. The statement issued by the State Department in January, 1950, that the Republic of South Korea, although it was established by the United Nations, was "not within our line of defense," was an open invitation to the North Korean Communists and to their Soviet and Chinese Communist allies to invade South Korea. The aggression of June 25, 1950, was its consequence. The Truman Administration's failure in the summer of 1945 to carry out Roosevelt's decision to set up a United Nations trusteeship for a unified Korea immediately after its liberation and the willingness of the White House and the State Department to sanction the Pentagon's decision to divide the country into two military zones made it all too easy for the propagandists in Moscow to create the impression in both Korea and China that South Korea was to become an American puppet state and an opening wedge for American imperialist expansion on the Asiatic mainland. It is only fair to recognize that both the Chinese and the Russians must consider the occupation of Korea by any alien power a threat, as each did in the years when it was occupied by Japan.

Whatever the military results of the United Nations campaign in Korea may be, the Western world faces the nightmare danger that before long an Iron Curtain may be down over East Asia and shut out all Western influence as rigidly as it is now excluded from Eastern Europe. Instead of seeing the rising tides of nationalism in Eastern Asia canalized into constructive channels with the help of the United States and the other Western democracies, there is now every indication that we will see them canalized into channels prepared for the people of Asia by the planners in Moscow. Then the immense manpower and material resources of the Far East will serve solely the interests of the Soviet Communist regime.

In contrast to our recent record in Europe and in the Far East, our national record within the United Nations has been almost invariably conducive to the development of collective security. President Truman has frequently announced that the United Nations has become the foundation of American foreign policy. This Government has generally lived up to that assurance in spirit and in act.

No more useful step could have been taken by the United States than that taken at the meeting of the General Assembly in the autumn of 1950. It was to me always inconceivable that that overwhelming majority of the members of the United Nations which sought neither expansion nor world domination, but desired solely to repress aggression, maintain world peace, advance the welfare of humanity, and strengthen the principle of collective security, would indefinitely permit the effective functioning of the United Nations Charter to be blocked by the Soviet veto within the Security Council. The solution was found when the United States, with the enthusiastic support of all but the Soviet Government and its satellites, secured the adoption by the General Assembly of a resolution containing this important principle: Should there be a threat to the peace of the world, a breach of the peace, or an act of aggression, and should the Security Council be then unable to take prompt action because of the imposition of a veto, the Assembly can be convened on twenty-four hours' notice by the vote of any seven members of the Security Council or by the vote of a majority of the sixty member nations of the Assembly.

The other provisions of the resolution adopted by the Assembly are almost as important as the basic principle. One provides for the creation of a "peace commission" to report on international tensions upon the request or consent of any individual country; another for the establishment by each member state of a national armed force trained, organized, and equipped to join immediately in collective action in case of aggression.

We now have the assurance that if the Security Council is unable to act to repress aggression, action can be taken by the General Assembly through the use of United Nations armed force. What has been demonstrated is that the Charter of the United Nations is elastic and subject to interpretation and amendment in precisely the same manner as the Constitution of the United States.

Since the reverses of the United Nations forces in Korea, the advocates of American isolation have been very vocal in their complaints that the brunt of the battle to liberate Korea has been borne by American troops, and that the troops of the other members of the United Nations have represented little more than token contingents. It is these same critics who are clamoring most loudly that the United States should do nothing further to help the countries of Western Europe unless they raise far larger armies of their own. And it is largely these same critics who have so bitterly opposed any financial or economic assistance to the peoples of Western Europe as a means of helping them contain the spread of communism. It hardly seems logical for them to propose that these countries should now, when the threat of Soviet attack is more serious than at any time since the end of the War, and they are being called upon for greatly increased military preparations and expenditures under the terms of the

Atlantic Defense Pact, reduce their present military establishments in Europe by sending large contingents to the Far East. To do so would only increase the likelihood that they will require greater military and financial help from the United States.

But this kind of unreasoning criticism is merely one evidence of the wave of hysteria that has swept over much of the United States since the Chinese Communist armies entered Korea, and the United Nations forces withdrew from the area above the 38th parallel.

The American people are facing what may well be the gravest national crisis that they have faced since the years of the Civil War. It is a time to close ranks. It is a time for cool and considered judgment. It is above all a time when our allies as well as our opponents should be shown that we are meeting the crisis with courage and with resolution and with a firm determination to persist in our effort to achieve collective security through the United Nations.

Yet it is precisely at this moment that the spokesmen for those isolationist policies which the history of the past thirty years has so clearly demonstrated to be fatal to the security of the United States and to the peace of the world urge upon us a form of neo-isolation that would be as pusillanimous as it would be disastrous to their own future safety.

Of these, ex-President Herbert Hoover is a typical example. With all due respect for Mr. Hoover's eminent qualities, and for the sincerity of his desire to serve his country's interests, I believe it would be difficult to find in the history of the United States a man who as President demonstrated less vision and less comprehension of how American influence might be best exercised in this nation's interest and in the interest of world peace, than Mr. Hoover did during those dark years of growing international crisis between 1929 and 1933. What Mr. Hoover has now urged upon his fellow citizens is tantamount to the scuttling of all forms of collective security, the cynical breach of all the obligations into which we have entered since 1945 to help other free peoples resist Soviet aggression, and the abandonment of all Europe (except perhaps Great Britain), all Asia, and presumably all Africa, to Soviet Communist control. If Mr. Hoover's advice were followed, it would mean that the United States would soon find herself without an ally in the world. Even the Republics of Latin America would lose all confidence in our willingness to abide by our promises in a moment of crisis. It would mean that war between the Soviet Union and the United States would become inevitable. And it would mean war under far worse conditions than those which now exist, since the Soviet Union would then possess all the vast industrial resources and strategic advantages that are now in the hands of the Western democracies. It would mean, even during the years that might intervene before a Soviet attack upon the Western Hemisphere, the slow but steady economic asphyxiation of the United States. For I doubt that even Mr. Hoover can imagine that a Soviet-dominated Europe, Asia and Africa would be permitted to trade with the nations of the New World.

Mr. Hoover's appeal could not have been more aptly characterized than it was in a broadcast by Elmer Davis. He termed it "a clarion call to his fellow countrymen to crawl under the bed, shut their eyes, plug their ears, and hope for the best."

Such counsels of abject defeatism are even more serious in their repercussions abroad than at home. It is not surprising that Mr. Hoover's address was published in full in the Soviet Union and in the Soviet satellite countries. Nothing could more effectively persuade the peoples behind the Iron Curtain that the American people were divided, and that Communist policies of aggression and of expansion would probably meet with no firm resistance by the United States. Nor is it surprising that in Western Europe, where determination to resist was never more needed, there is again uppermost in the mind of every man and woman the question whether the co-operation of the United States can really be depended upon or whether she will once more leave her fellow democracies to sink or swim, as she did in the years after the First World War.

Of course, one question is always asked in the case of any attempt such as this to appraise recent American foreign policy: Since you think that so much that we have done during the past five years and so much that we are doing at the present moment is mistaken or prejudicial, what should we now do to correct the errors that you have pointed out?

Necessarily, such a question cannot be answered with any glib assurance or except in general terms by anyone not in the councils of government. Much water has flowed over the dam since 1945, and as the title of this book indicates the decisions that were made yesterday shape the course of the events that are taking place today.

If our national policy, as I believe it will be, continues to be founded upon the United Nations, it would be a tragic mistake for us to acquiesce in any admission by the United Nations that the aggression of the North Korean Communists and of the Chinese Communists, aided and abetted by the Soviet Communists, can be permitted to achieve the ends that were sought. It would be an equally tragic mistake for us to let the Communist Government of China have a seat in the United Nations, unless and until it officially recognizes that it has been guilty of aggression, offers reparation for its acts of aggression, and agrees that a united people of Korea shall freely determine their own destinies under the auspices and supervision of the United Nations. It is not conceivable that a Government that has flagrantly violated so many of the basic principles set forth in the Preamble of the United Nations Charter could under existing conditions be admitted as a permanent member of the United Nations. Were the United States to take any other stand than this, she would be participating in a course of action that would fatally undermine the authority of the United Nations and bring about its destruction just as rapidly as the policies between 1931 and 1938 of the major powers within the League of Nations brought about the downfall of that international organization.

The United States should not consent to the return of Formosa to China until the United Nations has fully considered the best interests of the people of Formosa and all the political and military implications of such a step. She should in no event permit the cession of Formosa to China until and unless a recognized Chinese Government that has been admitted to the United Nations agrees to the establishment upon that island of the United Nations air and naval bases upon which President Roosevelt was so insistent.

If the United Nations and the United States take this stand, which is surely based upon our own enlightened national interest as well as upon principle, what policy should the United States then pursue in the Far East? Because present conditions throughout Asia are so uncertain, with the former friendly China rapidly becoming a Moscow-dominated and hostile power, the United States must, whatever the strain upon her national resources, maintain her defense outposts from the Aleutians through Japan, Okinawa, Formosa and the Philippines; and maintain them in such shape that Communist aggression against any part of our defense line can be successfully repelled.

Under these circumstances what would have seemed incredible in August, 1945, namely a partial rearmament of Japan, must be undertaken. It should be limited to what is required to enable the Japanese people to help in warding off any attack by the Asiatic Communists upon the Japanese home islands. Further, any rearmament should be under some form of continuing supervision by the United States. If the Soviet Government continues to oppose any reasonable terms for a final peace treaty with Japan, the treaty should be negotiated by the Western powers without further delay, so that the political anomalies and economic uncertainties resulting from an indefinite military occupation may be ended.

I believe it would be not only premature, but unrealistic, for the American people to assume that they can in the future count upon any sure support from the Japanese in a Western containment of Asiatic communism. "Asia for the Asiatics" is an eloquent slogan. It is a slogan that was first voiced during the Second World War by the Japanese themselves, and it has a legitimate appeal to all those Asiatic peoples who for so many generations have been subjected to Western imperialism. A sovereign and independent Japan will one day seek again to assume a position of leadership in Asia. Only if the Western powers try to rectify just grievances, to abolish the last remnants of colonialism, to remove discriminations based upon race or color, and to remedy those social and economic conditions which encourage communism, can we reasonably hope that Japan will seek to lead in promoting co-operation between the West and the East rather than join in that kind of fanatical exclusion of all Western influence upon which the present Communist Government of China seems so clearly bent.

In our relations with Europe we have but two alternatives: either to continue our economic assistance to the countries of Western Europe where it is still needed, continue military and economic assistance to Greece and to Turkey, and to expedite and facilitate the military preparedness of the members of the Atlantic Defense Pact; or to abandon all the advantages we have gained by these policies and permit the Soviet Union to take over Europe and the Near East whenever it sees fit.

If we adopt the second course, it is plain that our own bargaining position will be progressively weakened. Any hope of reaching an ultimate agreement with the Soviet Union must then be based upon our willingness to accept such terms as the Kremlin may dictate—and what those terms would be it is not difficult to imagine.

If the former alternative is adopted, there is still the likelihood that in any negotiations with the Soviet Union the bargaining position of the United States and of the other Western nations will be founded upon strength and not upon weakness.

I would also urge that in formulating our national foreign policy far more thought be given to our relations with our neighbors of the Western Hemisphere. At the time of our most dire need in 1942 the other American republics united behind us. In the years since the end of the war, they have far too often been excluded from our councils; and far too often their wholly justified requests for our co-operation in solving some of their more pressing economic and financial difficulties have been ignored. It seems to be difficult for many of those now in authority in Washington to understand that the assistance we give our neighbors in the Western Hemisphere in developing their natural resources, raising their living standards, and promoting industrialization is of as much benefit to us as it is to them. Industrialization, the development of natural resources and the rise of living standards mean increased purchasing power, and hence the increased consumption in peacetime of American exports. At the same time they help to eliminate the social conditions that are peculiarly conducive to the spread of Communist propaganda. Finally, they increase the capacity of our neighbors to provide us with strategic materials and other forms of practical help in wartime.

It might as well be recognized that since the end of the Second World War the other American republics have felt increasingly that our devotion to inter-American solidarity is far more noticeable when the United States faces an international emergency than it is during more normal times.

The policy thus roughly outlined is obviously a policy of containment—containment by military force and by economic power of a Soviet Union that has shown every intention of expanding its hegemony in Europe, in Asia and in the Near East. It is necessarily a negative policy designed to serve the basic purpose of self-defense as long as the period of international crisis continues. However, it should in my opinion be inseparably linked to more positive and constructive policies. One of these is President Truman's Point Four Program of technical and expert assistance to the more backward and undeveloped peoples. Another would be a policy of expertly conducted propaganda, using every means of communication available to convince the people in every country of the world of our peaceful purposes and of the individual blessings to be gained through a world order founded upon the repression of aggression, the consecration of individual liberty and of human rights, and the promotion of economic security. Finally, we should make it unmistakably clear that the United States is always willing to negotiate with the Soviet Union whenever her acts match her professions of peaceful intent.

The American people have never before faced the necessity of persisting in a foreign policy that requires time, patience and unlimited sacrifice if it is to be successful. They have never before had to envisage the possibility of having to put up with continued tension and recurrent mobilization, both military and economic, over a period of many years. Yet I see no way now of avoiding this necessity if the safety of the United States is to be assured. If war is avoided, and we Americans persist year in and year out in such a policy, there is the chance that little by little the Iron Curtain will rust away and that the peoples of the East and of the West can eventually work together as partners in the United Nations.

But whatever foreign policy this Government may devise, there is no more urgent need than that it be known by every other nation of the world to be dependable. How can the influence of the United States be used effectively unless the other countries have faith that our commitments will be carried out, and that the co-operation we offer today will not be replaced by a return to isolation tomorrow? If we are to give any real assurance of our national dependability, American foreign policy must become truly bipartisan, as it was to so large a degree during those years when Arthur H. Vandenberg magnificently served this country's highest interests in the Senate of the United States.

If American foreign policy, and in particular our national pledge to found that policy upon the United Nations, become partisan issues, the bitter sacrifices that the American people have made during the past decade will prove to have been made in vain.

In the great contest that is being waged between the free nations who would preserve human liberty and the Communist tyranny that would destroy every vestige of human liberty, the Soviet Union could anticipate no greater advantage than to find the American people timid, hesitant and confused, weakened by divided councils, and unwilling to persevere in their search for a free and peaceful world along the road upon which they set their feet at San Francisco in 1945.

Index

Advisory Committee on Post-War Foreign Policy in Department of State, 133
Alexander I of Russia, 145
American Foreign Ministers, Conference of (see Rio de Janeiro Conference)
American Foreign Service, 216
American Red Cross, 20, 45, 51, 54
Anglo-French Commercial Treaty, 11
Anglo-German Naval Treaty (1935), 3
Anti-Comintern Pact (1936), 69
Aranha, Dr. Oswaldo, 102, 108-110, 112, 120
Argentina, 98-100, 105-120
 and Brazil, rivalry between, 100-101
 and Chile, 112, 114, 118
 isolation policy of, 102
Argentine Army, influence of, on Argentina's national policy, 100, 101
Argentine Constitution in 1942, similarity of, to U.S. Constitution, 112
Armistice Day proposal, 22-30
 advantages of, 18-19
 formulation of, 16-18
Armstrong, Hamilton Fish, 183
Asia, rise of nationalism in, 147
Atlantic Charter, 124, 127, 129, 130, 175, 181
 American enthusiasm for, 180
Atlantic Charter meeting (1941), 86, 89, 178
Atlantic Defense Pact, 212-213, 223, 228
Attlee, Clement, 175, 205
Austin, Sen. Warren, 183
Axis, Latin American relations with, 94-122
Axis Pact (1940), 82

Baldwin, Hanson W., 159-161, 163, 164
Baldwin, Stanley, 2, 70, 71, 170
 on rearmament of Germany, 3
Baltic states, and peace settlements, 129, 135-137, 142
Barthou, Louis, 3
Behind the Ballots, 61
Beneš, Eduard, 130-132
Bevin, Ernest, 205
Blum, Léon, 59
Bolivia, 99, 102, 108, 113, 116, 119
Bowman, Dr. Isaiah, 183
Brazil, 98, 99, 106, 108-111, 113, 115-118, 120, 121
 and Argentina, rivalry between, 100-101
 foreign policy of, 101, 102
 U.S. airfields in, 121
Brest-Litovsk, Treaty of, 143, 214
British Foreign Office, 48
British Information Service, 47
British Intelligence, 47, 49
Brussels Conference on the Far East (1937), 16, 29, 74-75, 92
Buenos Aires Conference (1936), 8, 9, 67, 103-104, 180
 objectives of, 103

Byrnes, James F., 206-209
 "mission to Moscow" of, 207-209

Cairo Conference (1943), 137, 147, 149, 191, 216
Camacho, Pres. Avila, 189
Castillo, Dr. Ramon S., 100, 101
Central America, support for Western Allies in, 98
Chaco war, 99, 103
Chamberlain, Neville, 15, 23, 25-30, 71, 72
Chiang Kai-shek, 87, 137, 147, 148, 161, 170, 216, 217, 219
 aid to, 67
 and Roosevelt, 151, 155
 and Stalin, 169
 and Stilwell, feud between, 155
 (See also Nationalist Government, Chinese)
Chiang Kai-shek, Madame, 152, 216
Chicago Daily News, 115
Chile, 96-99, 106, 108, 109, 111, 112, 119, 120
 and Brazil, relations between, 101
 neutrality of, 100
China, 151-153, 161
 currency problem of, 67-68
 invasion of, by Japan, 7, 8, 69-71, 147
 (See also Chiang Kai-shek; Chinese Communists; Nationalist Government)
Chinese Communists, 147, 148, 151, 152, 156, 217, 228
Churchill, Winston, 3, 27, 28, 30, 32, 36, 41, 45-48, 62, 63, 81, 86, 128, 129, 137, 139, 150, 152, 159, 170, 205
 and De Gaulle, 47
 on German rearmament, 215
 on postwar problems, 187-188
 and Roosevelt, 199
  on China, 154, 161
  at Tehran Conference (see Tehran Conference)
 and Truman, 202-203
 on United Nations organization, 172, 173, 175
 at Yalta (see Yalta Conference)
Cobden, Richard, 11-12
Cohen, Benjamin V., 183
Colombia, 96, 102, 108
Communism, Soviet, 218-219
Communist propaganda, in Asia, 148, 149
 in China, 219
 in France, 31
Conference of American Foreign Ministers (see Rio de Janeiro Conference)
Congressional Pearl Harbor Investigating Committee, 86-87
Connally, Sen. Tom, 183
Coolidge, Calvin, 6, 180
Costa Rica, 96
Council of Foreign Ministers, 206-207
Curzon Line, 142

Czechoslovakia, 5, 210
  American forces in, 202-203
  postwar peace settlements for, 131, 132

Dairen, 138, 153, 159, 160, 162
Daladier, Édouard, 59
Daniels, Jonathan, 219
Danish Merchant Marine, and Great
  Britain, 49
Darlan, Adm. Jean, 37
  Vice Premier, 50, 53, 64
Davis, Elmer, 224
Davis, Norman H., 20-21, 23, 25, 75, 76,
  183
De Gaulle, Gen. Charles, 36, 187
  and Churchill, 47
  St. Pierre and Miquelon seized by, 62-63
Deutscher, I., 141
Disarmament Conference of 1933, 67
Duggan, Laurence, 115
Dumbarton Oaks, 185, 191, 192, 195
Dupuy, of Canada, 46

ECA, 210
Economic Warfare, Board of, 183, 184
Ecuador, 96, 99, 102, 108, 113, 116, 120
Eden, Anthony, 10, 27, 48, 71, 75, 91, 205
  and Stalin, 126-129, 138, 141, 199-200
  visit to America, on postwar problems,
    186-188
"Eight Pillars of Peace," 8-10
Eisenhower, Dwight D., 174
Espil, Argentine Ambassador, 104
Estigarribia, Gen. Jose Felix, 99
European Advisory Commission, 137
Executive Committee, 18, 19

Far Eastern Policy, before Pearl Harbor,
  66-93
  from Pearl Harbor to Hiroshima, 146-171
  since 1945, 216-228
  (See also Roosevelt, Far Eastern policy of)
Farley, James A., 61
Faulhaber, Gen. von, 102
Feis, Herbert, 70, 79, 85
Finland, 5
Flandin, Pierre Étienne, 4, 50
Foch, Marshal Ferdinand, 34
Foreign Relations Committee of the Senate,
  125, 161
Formosa, 148, 152-153, 226
Fourteen Points, 123, 124
France, 1-5
  fear of German rearmament in, 211-213
  and Great Britain, 45
  hostility of, toward Great Britain, 35-37
  Vichy Government of, recognition of, 31-
    65
  Vichy policy, 123
Franco, Francisco, 100
  and Hitler, 32, 37-38
Free French, 31, 36, 47-48, 62, 63
French Indo-China, 82-84
French North Africa, 52
French resistance, 55-56
Fulbright resolution, 173

Gasperi, Alcide de, 217
Gathering Storm, The, 27, 28, 30

General Assembly of the United Nations,
  peace commission of, 222
  resolution of, in 1950, 221, 222
  Soviet Union in, 175
  votes in, 194
Germany, 15
  attack of, on Soviet Union, 54-55
  occupation of, 202-206
  rearmament of, 3
    fear of, in Western Europe, 211-215
  (See also Hitler, Adolf)
Goebbels, Joseph P., 3, 55
Goering, Hermann, 3
Good Neighbor Policy, 98
Grand Alliance, The, 63, 128, 175
Great Britain, 1, 2, 4, 31
  policy of, three objectives of, 2
  and Soviet Union, on postwar peace
    settlements, 126-131
  (See also Churchill, Winston)
Great Mistakes of the War, 159
"Greater Argentina," doctrine of, 101
Guani, Dr., of Uruguay, 108
Guiñazú, Dr. Ruiz, 100, 109
Gunther, John, 173

Halifax, Lord, 48, 49, 188
Harding, Warren G., 5, 180
Hawaii, 109
Hayden, Allen, 115
Hitler, Adolf, 14, 15, 175, 181, 218
  air attack of, on Great Britain, 36
  and Austria, 28, 29
  and Franco, 32, 37-38
  and Mussolini, 57
  occupation of Rhineland by, 4, 50
  policies of, 8
Hoare, Sir Samuel, 70
Hoffman, Paul, 210
Hoover, Herbert, 6, 7, 180
  isolationism of, 223-225
  and Latin America, 103
Hopkins, Harry, 89-91, 159, 163
  isolationism of, 179
  talks with Stalin, 166
Hornbeck, Dr. Stanley, 216
Hu-Shih, Dr., 87, 218, 219
Hull, Cordell, 8-13, 15, 20, 83, 183, 184, 188
  antipathy of, to Argentina, 104-105
  book of reminiscences, 117-119
  and Chinese, 88
  "Eight Pillars of Peace" of, 8-10
  and Free French, 62-63
  on Japan, 70
  negotiations of, with Japanese, 86-90
  opposition of, to Buenos Aires Confer-
    ence, 103
    to peace project, 21-26, 29, 30
    to Rio de Janeiro Conference, 115-120
  on postwar settlements, 126-127
  reaction of, to criticism, 61
  and Roosevelt, 51-64
    friction between, 135
  Trade Agreements Act of 1934, 11, 12

I Was There, 32, 164
Ickes, Harold, 73, 84
Indo-China, French, 82-84
  Japan in, 55

Intelligence Service, U.S., in Latin America, 121
Inter-American Conference for the Maintenance of Peace (*see* Buenos Aires Conference)
Inter-American Conference of 1939 in Panama, 105
Intergovernmental Committee on Refugees (1938), 67
International Organization, Departmental Committee on, 184
Iran, and Soviet Union, 193
Isolationism, American, 5-7, 15, 73, 76, 177, 180, 222, 223

Japan, 15
 defeat of, 146
 fishing fleets of, Roosevelt's project concerning, 76-77
 and French Indo-China, 82-84
 invasion of China by, 7, 8, 69-71, 147
 invasion of Manchuria by, 67, 69, 70, 75, 91
 military occupation of, 146-147
 "moral embargo" on, 79-80
 rearmament of, 227
 shipments of oil, scrap iron and steel to, 79-82
 Treaty of Commerce and Navigation with, 80
 truce proposal to, 87-88
 war with, 156-158
Japanese invasion, danger of, to United States, 96
Japanese invasion force in Camranh Bay, 83
Japanese policy in 1940, 79
Justo, Gen. Augustin, 101, 110

Kellogg Pact, 9
Kerenski regime in Russia, 144
King, MacKenzie, 46
Knox, Frank, 81, 82
Konoye, Prince, 71
Korea, 153, 167-169, 219-220
 fighting in, 93
 and United Nations, 147-149, 174, 193, 220, 226
 United Nations forces in, 222, 223
Kurile Islands, 138, 153, 159, 162
Kurusu, Adm. Saburo, 86

Langer, William L., 32, 41, 60, 64
Latin America, feelings of, toward United States, 98
 relations of, with Axis, 94-122
Laval, Pierre, 3, 35, 37
 and Hitler, 37-38
 and Pétain, 50, 51
League of Nations, failure of, 1, 5, 173, 174, 177, 195, 226
 and Great Britain, 70
 and Japan, 169
 Roosevelt on, 176-177
Leahy, Adm. William D., 32, 42, 206, 219
 Ambassador to France, 43-46, 50, 53, 54, 56

Leahy, Adm. William D.—*Continued*
 Chief of Naval Operations, 72, 74
 Governor of Puerto Rico, 43
 and Pétain, 51, 57, 58
 recall of, from France, 59, 60
 on war with Japan, 157, 158
 on Yalta agreements, 164-165
Léger, Alexis, 35
Lend-Lease, 55
 to Russia, 141, 143
Lenin, Nikolai, 131, 142, 144, 166, 218
Lindsay, Sir Ronald, 26-27
Lippmann, Walter, 123-125
"Little Cabinet" of Wilson Administration, 20
Litvinoff, Maksim, 143
Lloyd George, David, 3
London Economic Conference (1933), 6, 16, 23

MacArthur, Gen. Douglas, 146
McCormick, Anne O'Hare, 183
MacDonald, Ramsay, 2, 176
Maginot Line, 3
Man of Independence, The, 219
Manchuria, 67, 69, 70, 75, 91
Marshall, Gen. George C., 81, 106
 in China, 217, 219
 Secretary of State, on China, 170
 on war with Japan, 157, 158
Marshall Plan, 210-211
Matthews, Freeman, 40
Mein Kampf, 218
Mers el Kebir, French warships attacked by British at, 35-36, 45
Mexico, 96, 108, 112
Milyukov, Prof. Pavel, 144
Missouri, U.S.S., 146, 148
Molotov, Vyacheslav, 126, 128, 130
Montoire Conference between Pétain and Hitler, 39, 46, 50
Morgenthau, Henry, 73
Morley, John, 11
Moscow Conference (1943), 137
Mountbatten, Lord Louis, 146
Murphy, Robert, 52
Mussolini, Benito, 15, 181
 invasion of Abyssinia by, 70, 75
 policies of, 8

Nationalist Government, Chinese, 68, 147, 148, 151, 152, 154-156, 161, 162, 169, 170, 217-218
 and United States, friction between, 87-88
Nazis, 5
Netherlands East Indies, 89-91, 150
Neutrality Act, 69, 80
Neutrality legislation toward Spain, 76
New Deal, first "Hundred Days" of, 66
Nine Power Treaty, 75, 93
Nine Powers, 92
Nomura, Adm. Kichisaburo, 83, 86
North Africa, 57, 58, 60
 French, 52
Norway, 150
Nuremberg trials, 28
Nye Committee, 6

Okinawa, 146
On Active Service in Peace and War, 74, 195
Open Door policy, 171
Organization of the American States, 118, 184
Ortiz, Dr. Roberto, 100, 101, 110
Our Vichy Gamble, 32, 41, 60

Padilla, Dr., of Mexico, 94, 112
Panama Canal, safety of, importance of, 95, 96
Pan-American Conference of 1938 at Lima, 103, 105
Panay, attack on, 74
Paraguay, 99, 102, 108, 113, 116, 119
Paris Peace Conference (1919), 124-126
Peace project, 16-30
    and Great Britain, 26-27
Peace settlements, postponement of, 123-145
Pearl Harbor, attack on, 58, 98, 181
    damage at, 95
Pearson, Drew, 94
Pearson, Mrs. Drew, 94
Pennsylvania, University of, 119
Pérez, Dr. Parra, 112
Pershing, Gen. John J., 34, 42
Peru, 96, 99, 102, 108, 113, 116, 119
Peruvian-Ecuadorean boundary dispute, 115
Pétain, Henri, 34-37, 43-45, 55-56
    and Darlan, 55, 56, 58
    and Hitler, 31, 33
        at Montoire Conference, 39, 46, 50
    and Laval, 37, 40, 59
    and Roosevelt, 39-41, 58, 59
Pilsudski, Józef, 5, 35
Point Four Program, 229
Poland, 5
    and peace settlements, 127, 130-132
Portsmouth, Treaty of, 153
Potsdam Conference, 145, 166, 199-207
Prado, Dr. Manuel, 108
Press, U.S., at Rio de Janeiro Conference, 107, 109, 114, 115
Propaganda, 31-32
    (*See also* Communist propaganda)

"Quarantine," naval barrier, 8, 13
"Quarantine" speech (*see* Roosevelt, "quarantine" speech of)
Quebec Conference, second (1944), 157, 160

Reber, Samuel, 63
Reciprocal Trade Agreements, 98
Reynaud, Paul, 36
Ribbentrop Plan, 78
Rio de Janeiro Conference (1942), 63, 94, 102-104, 106-108, 122
    formula at, 114
    Hull's opposition to, 115-120
    Mediation Commission of, 115
    Political Committee of, 114
Riom, trials at, 59
Road to Pearl Harbor, The, 70, 79, 85
Roberts Report, 90

Roosevelt, Eleanor, 132, 138, 179
Roosevelt and Hopkins, 64, 89-90, 189
Roosevelt in Retrospect, 173
Roosevelt, Franklin D., 125, 126, 202-204, 217, 219, 220, 226
    "Arsenal of democracy" speech of, 55
    attitude of, toward small countries, 178
    and Chiang Kai-shek, 151
        friction between, 155
    and China, 67-69
        on China as major power, 186-187, 190
    and Churchill, Atlantic Charter meeting of, 178
        on French disarmament, 187
        on Japan, 157, 158
        at Yalta (*see* Yalta Conference)
    on Communism, 198
    concern of, with foreign affairs, 66-67
    Far Eastern policy of, 149-153, 169-171
    on Far Eastern postwar settlements, 154, 159, 161, 164
    formulating of Armistice Day appeal, 16-18
    on France as major power, 186, 187
    on German disarmament, 215
    and Hull, 61-64
        friction between, 135
    idiosyncrasies of, 215-216
    and Japan, 71-93
        trade embargo proposal, 71-72, 74, 76, 92
    on League of Nations, 176-177
    personality of, 77-78
    and Pétain, 39-41, 58, 59
    and postwar peace settlements, 130, 133-134, 136
        plebiscites idea, 136
    preoccupation of, with role as wartime leader, 135, 145, 179
    "quarantine" speech of, 13, 21, 24, 72, 76, 91-93
    reforming of Supreme Court, 7
    and Rio de Janeiro Conference, 116-117, 120, 122
    on security of British and French fleets, 33-34
    Soviet people's opinion of, 140
    and Stalin, 136-137, 191, 192, 194
        at Tehran (*see* Tehran Conference)
    on United Nations organization, 172-176, 197-198
    for universal reduction of armaments, 6
    and Vargas, 110, 111
    and Vichy policy, 60, 65
        reactions of, to criticism on, 60-61
    and Weygand, 58
    at Yalta (*see* Yalta Conference)
Rossetti, Dr., of Chile, 100

Saavedra Lamas, Dr. Carlos, 104, 105
Saavedra Lamas Antiwar Pact, 9
Sakhalin, 138, 153, 159, 162
Schuman Plan, 211-213
Security Council of the United Nations, 133, 185
    Soviet Union in, 149, 174, 175, 192, 193
    veto of, 221
Sherwood, Robert, 64, 89-90, 189, 190

Sikorski, Gen. Wladyslaw, 130-131
Silver Purchase Act of 1934, 67, 68
Simms, William Philip, 94
Simon, Sir John, 70
Soong, T. V., 87, 88
South America, Axis relations with, 97-122
  opinion of Hitler in, 97
Soviet Revolution, 11
Soviet Union, policy of, since Potsdam Conference, 201-231
  and postwar peace claims, 125-126, 134, 137-145
    Baltic states, 129, 135-137, 142
    Far East, 138, 153, 159-161, 163, 164
    Poland, 127, 130, 131, 135
  and United States, relations between, 165, 166, 168
  (*See also* Stalin, Joseph)
Spain, neutrality legislation toward, 76
Spanish Civil War, 14
Stalin, Joseph, 126, 128, 129, 131, 132, 141-144, 181, 189, 201
  and China, 161-162, 169
  and Churchill, 191
  on Far East, 218
  foreign policy of, 165-167
  and Hitler, 131, 199-200
    (*See also* Stalin-Hitler pact)
  and Roosevelt, 136-137
  at Tehran (*see* Tehran Conference)
  on United Nations organization, 172, 173
  at Yalta (*see* Yalta Conference)
Stalin-Hitler pact (1939), 78, 125, 128, 129, 142
Stark, Adm. Harold, 81, 83, 106
State Department, Advisory Committee on Post-War Foreign Policy in, 133
  postwar research work by, 182-187, 189
Stilwell, Gen. Joseph, and Chiang Kai-shek, feud between, 155
Stimson, Henry L., 7, 66, 73, 74, 81, 82, 96
  policy of, on Japan, 67
  on United Nations, 195-197
Submarine menace, 95-96

Taylor, Myron C., 183
Taylor, Wayne, 94
Tehran Conference, 137, 138, 140, 142, 145, 149, 165, 174, 176, 189-191, 204
Thailand, and Japan, 82
Their Finest Hour, 45
Time for Decision, The, 27
Tojo Cabinet, 86
Trade Agreements Act of 1934, 11, 12
Treasury Department aid to Chiang Kai-shek, 67
Treaty of Commerce and Navigation with Japan, 80
Truman, Harry S., 149, 163, 203-205, 217, 219-221
  Point Four Program of, 229

United Nations, 12, 118, 124, 125, 221
  China in, 225-226
  creation of, 172-198

United Nations—*Continued*
  formation of, at Tehran Conference, 190
  and Formosa, 148
  General Assembly of (*see* General Assembly of the United Nations)
  and Korea (*see* Korea, and United Nations)
  need for, 92-93
  policy formed by, 223, 225, 231
  Security Council of (*see* Security Council of the United Nations)
  Soviet Union in, 164, 169, 192, 197
  structure of, 183-184
  veto right in, 185
United Nations Charter, 92, 148, 174, 176, 196, 200, 221, 222, 226
United Nations Declaration, 124, 129
United States, Europe's lack of faith in, 206, 207, 209-210
  foreign policy of, since 1945, 201-231
  and French North Africa, 52
  policy of, on aggression, 15
    in Europe, since 1945, 201-216, 228
    in Far East (*see* Far Eastern policy)
    in South America, since 1945, 228-229
    toward Vichy Government, 60, 64-65
  political influence of, 140
  production supremacy of, 140, 141
United States diplomacy, objectives of, concerning Vichy Government, 33-35
Uruguay, 98-99, 102, 108, 116, 119

Vandenburg, Arthur H., 230
Vargas, Getulio, 101, 102, 110, 111, 113, 114
Venezuela, 102, 108, 112
Versailles Treaty, 4
Veto right in United Nations, 185, 192, 193
Vichy Government, recognition of, 31-65
Vichy policy, 123
Vienna, Congress of (1815), 126, 145
Vishinsky, Andrei, 209

Wallace, Henry, 73, 183
Washington Naval Treaty (1922), 74
  Japan's withdrawal from, 69
Wedemeyer, Gen., 170
Welles, Sumner, Acting Secretary of State, 81, 83
  delegate at Inter-American Conference of 1939, 105
  on Far Eastern policy, 162
  Under Secretary of State, 8, 14
Weygand, Gen. Maxime, 46, 52, 56, 57
Whitaker, Arthur P., 119
Wilhelmina of the Netherlands, 150
Wilson, Woodrow, 136, 195
  Fourteen Points of, 123, 124
Winant, Amb. John G., 126

Yalta agreements, 162-165
Yalta Conference, 137, 138, 145, 149, 156, 158-160, 165, 170, 174, 193, 204, 208, 209, 216
  Far Eastern agreements at, 147
Yokohama Bay, 146